DECORATING
FURNITURE

DECORATING FURNITURE

Simple techniques · Imaginative ideas

Jo-an Jenkins

G. P. PUTNAM'S SONS/NEW YORK

A Design Press Book

Copyright © 1984 Jo-an Jenkins

Library of Congress Catalog Card Number 84-60635
ISBN 0-399-13010-1
Printed in Spain

CONTENTS

INTRODUCTION

Like Cinderella's pumpkin before it became a coach, the lowliest, most ordinary piece of furniture—an old office desk or filing cabinet, a junk shop table or chest from Auntie Jane—can turn into an amusing, even beautiful object for you to use and enjoy every day. The change is almost magical and, best of all, the simple skills needed to decorate furniture with wit and charm can be learned quickly and easily. Imagination is all you need.

The cleverest techniques come from professional designers and decorators. For them, time is money and so they've developed simple, often makeshift methods for achieving imaginative and delightful decorative effects with the least amount of effort. Of course, there are skilled craftsmen who spend years polishing the complicated techniques needed to reproduce intricately detailed surfaces like porphyry and boulle, bois and malachite, but for most of us, this is only a distant dream.

Happily, it doesn't matter as there is an almost endless variety of enchanting decorative effects which can be created by even the least skilled and nimble-fingered. Most use paint in a number of ways, but torn or cut paper pasted on in découpage or collage also offers an effective medium for transformation. And since these techniques come from professionals, they are swift and simple to do.

Everything in this book can be learned with only a short practice session. Nothing takes more than one or two (or, at the most, three) steps beyond the basic ground coat of colour and the final protective layer of polyurethane varnish. The production of a piece does take time in that each coating of paint must be allowed to dry thoroughly before proceeding to the next step, but the actual time spent working at each session can be measured in minutes rather than hours.

Of course, you can take much more time and devote far more skill by combining several techniques. For example, you could spatter over sponging and then add a stencil on top, or sponge in one colour and rag roll in a second, followed by a slight spatter to finish. It all depends on you.

But the main aim of this book is to excite and inspire. There are people who like cookbooks to savour, taking joy in the reading, and those who like every measurement and temperature spelled out in detail, lest the soufflé fall. This book lies somewhere in between, detailed enough to introduce each technique and flexible enough to encourage you to launch out on your own. The decorative effects you create can be just as pleasing and interesting as any in the book.

This book is just a beginning: you take it from here.

BEFORE BEGINNING

What Can I Do?

Any solid, well-shaped piece of furniture can take on new life with a bit of spirited decorating: the ungainly old wardrobe from granny's attic, finds from the local junk shop or second-hand furniture auction, boring basics from the local furniture store, even second-hand office equipment. And don't forget the kitchen. Basic do-it-yourself units or metal cabinets inherited from the previous cook can be given a customized finish worthy of the chicest of professional interior decorators—even the refrigerator can be worked into the scheme.

There are just a few, key questions to ask:
- Is it sturdy, well-made and in generally good condition?
- Will it do the job I need it to do?
- Is the basic shape acceptable to me?
- Is it good value for money?

If the answer to all of these is yes, then the piece is probably worth the time and care needed to renew it successfully. Minor damages, like loose chair stretchers or a broken hinge, are easily repaired and more serious problems, such as missing feet or mouldings, must be judged according to your own willingness and ability to do the woodwork involved. Other small amounts of carpentry—removing the mirror from a dresser or adding feet to raise the height of a chest—may turn a marginal piece of furniture into the right one. Judging any candidate for decorating should allow for these possibilities.

There are, however, certain important things to avoid:
- Never restore or decorate anything which might be valuable or classified as an antique. If it looks like a fine, well-made piece of furniture, always ask an expert before doing any work on it at all. Most pieces are worth more in their original, possibly damaged state than when repaired, and

Below left: a junk shop desk turns into a pretty dressing table when painted a soft colour and covered with delicately brushed ferns. Below right: a lined border finishes it off neatly.

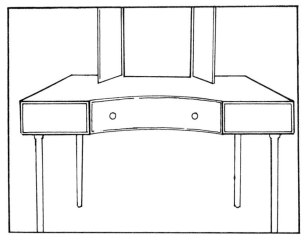
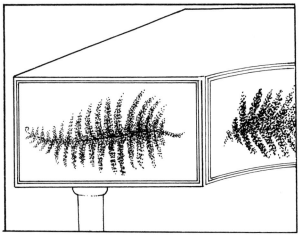

even an old painted piece might be worth a considerable amount because of its decorative finish.

- Never touch anything with traces of woodworm. It's death to furniture and can easily spread to floors and other wooden surfaces. It can be identified by powdery wood dust and tiny round holes. Very mild cases can be treated with proprietory woodworm solutions, but advanced cases need professional care.
- Avoid anything with loose joints in any quantity, tide-marked wood indicating exposure to damp and panels with broad cracks in them. Keep a sharp eye out for fungi too. Your nose should learn to tell the difference between the musty and the merely dusty.
- Steer clear, too, of metal rods or wires, visibly placed screws and clumsy repair jobs that have destroyed the original character of the piece.
- In metal office furniture, avoid items with moving parts that no longer operate properly, unless you are sure that a drop of oil is all they need. Missing or broken hinges will be difficult to restore as most are welded on rather than fastened with nuts and bolts.

Although most of your second-hand furniture finds will be tables, chairs, chests of drawers, desks or wardrobes, please don't limit your hunting to these categories alone. Trolleys and shelves, and small items such as metal or wooden lamps and trays are equally good candidates for decorating. With imagination, old plan chests and school trunks can become coffee tables and an old television or filing cabinet can act as a side table next to a bed or sofa.

Even chipboard can be used to create furniture for decorating. Unable to afford a larger dining-room table, one clever lady simply ordered the right size cut in chipboard at the local timber yard, fixed braces on the bottom to hold it in place on top of her existing table, and then faux marbled the new top to match the walls. A leading London decorator takes that idea even further, ordering round chipboard tables made to her own specifications and then painting an elaborate inlaid marble pattern on the top of each one.

Below left: a secondhand coffee table. Below right: it makes an amusing centrepiece when striped with bands of colour stroked on with a thick, felt-tip pen, or fully loaded artist's brush.

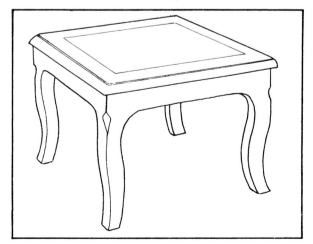

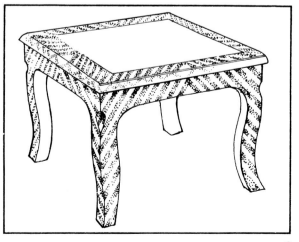

Basic Cleaning and Repairing

When a newly bought piece of junk furniture arrives home, put it wherever you plan to work on it and examine it thoroughly. Any dirt or grime will need to be scrubbed away, but not with soapy water. Water is bad for wood in every possible way; either the wood will become flexible and warp, or become damp and begin to rot, or, at the very least, the wet will make the grain rise, adding to the job of sanding and smoothing the surface preparatory to painting.

If the piece is only slightly dirty, a well squeezed-out sponge and mild dishwashing detergent may be enough to clean it. If the wood is painted or varnished or french polished, any proprietory paint cleaner will help clean it thoroughly. If there is any veneer, be particularly careful not to let moisture or solvent get underneath, as this may lift the veneer further, creating a fiddly repair job. Always work with the least amount of moisture or solvent as possible. Encrusted dirt or plaster should come off with fine sandpaper or wire wool.

Sticky old varnish should be stripped away completely with a proprietory paint stripper. A very light coating can be removed very simply with fine wire wool or sandpaper.

Once your piece is completely clean and dry, repairs can be made. If you have been sensible, these should be fairly easy.

There are several excellent do-it-yourself books on the market which give detailed guides to woodworking tools and repairs of every kind. While this book does not pretend to offer the same coverage of what is a very complicated and varied subject, a brief guide to what you might need can be very useful. Even the least dedicated do-it-yourselfer can manage a few repairs with a minimum of skill.

Scraping Tools
There are several simple tools which can be used by themselves or in combination with chemical paint strippers to smooth wood surfaces or built-up layers of thick paint and varnish.

The cabinet scraper is the most essential tool—a fine, flexible sheet of toughened steel. It is held in both hands and tilted forwards slightly as it is pushed away from your body, taking off shaving after shaving of a uniformly fine thickness of nearly the same width as the blade. The finish left on the wood is so smooth that only a rub with the finest abrasive paper is needed before it is ready for painting.

The broad scraper is a semi-flexible knife with a flat, 3in (75mm) blade for removing paint, varnish etc.

The putty knife (or filling knife) is a slightly narrower, more flexible knife used for applying wood fillers, etc.

The combination shave hook is a handy extra tool with a

combination of curves, points and angles, etc, for removing varnish and paint from crevices and curved surfaces.

Shaping and Smoothing Tools
A few tools will be required for smoothing and rounding edges and corners as well as flat surfaces.

Planes reduce wood or filler, making it flat and smooth. The two most useful are the jack plane, designed for general use and the block plane which is smaller and narrower and can be held in one hand. It is useful for working in small areas and trimming the end grain. Blades on good planes are expensive, but can be reground. Beware hidden screws and nails or else get a plane with cheap, replaceable blades.

Files and rasps help to shape corners and edges swiftly and neatly. Two or three are all that is needed: a coarse rasp for heavier smoothing, a fine rattail file for crevices and curves, and a milled file in its own holder for more general filing.

Carving Tools
These are not for serious carving, but to cut small braces for sagging drawers or to insert in loose legs or shelves. It may also be necessary to cut or enlarge holes for some repairs, and carving them out is the quickest and simplest method.

Chisels (straight-edged) and **gouges** (round-edged) are efficient and sharp cutting tools, potentially very dangerous unless, paradoxically, they are kept razor sharp. It is when they are dulled that they may slip and cause damage. Chisels cut rounder, deeper curves, while gouges are used for shallower carving. Both normally need sharpening when new. They are hit with a wooden mallet to control the direction and depth of the cut. A hammer is too heavy and risks accidents.

Hammers
It is handy to have one fairly large and solid hammer for heavy work and a smaller, lighter hammer for tapping in small tacks and nails. Both should be claw hammers with a curving hook for removing unwanted nails (always put a small block of wood under the front end to protect the wood). You will also need to have a wooden hammer or mallet for chiselling.

Saws and Drills
A panel saw is needed for larger planks and a tenon saw for more accurate work. An electric drill is invaluable, with or without attachments, but is too bulky for some jobs. A hand drill is essential for fine and delicate drilling.

Clamps and Vices
Clamps and vices are used to hold things firmly in place while you work on them and are particularly necessary when gluing, as the loose piece must be held tightly until the glue is dry. A multipurpose vice is undoubtedly the most useful as it can be adjusted to a variety of sizes and positions, but two or three separate clamps can serve your needs equally well.

Extras

A good steel tape rule for measuring is another basic that should be in any tool box. Heavy plastic gloves and barrier creams protect your hands when using strippers or any other chemicals. Inexpensive breathing masks are wise when you are doing a lot of sanding or filing. Wood filler and a good woodworking glue, such as PVA adhesive or Urea, are useful. Finally, a supply of various weights of sandpaper and wire wool will be needed for smoothing a surface before painting.

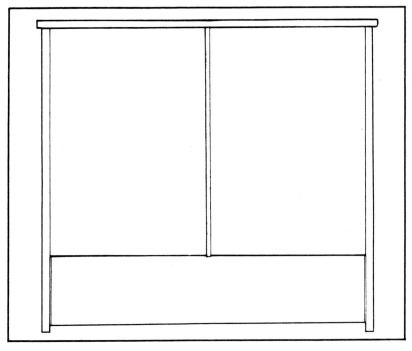

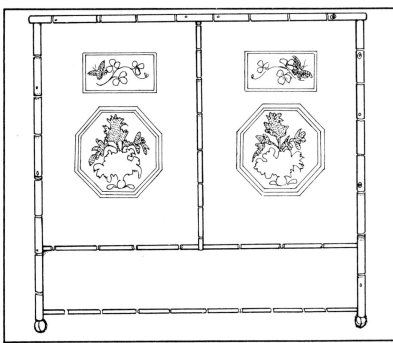

Reshaping Furniture 1
Above right: plain television cab-
inet, practical but boring.
Below right: the same cabinet with
added wheel-around castors, glued-
on moulding trim and bouquets of
painted flowers.

Reshaping Furniture

A particular chest of drawers may look better without the mirror fixed on top. Another chest might be ideal if only it had legs which lifted it up a little more—or, if the legs came off, lowering the top so that it fitted as a table next to the bed. Either way, simple carpentry like this is within anyone's skill.

Taking off: If you want to remove legs or a miror or any other embellishments that spoil the shape of a piece of furniture—first look to see how they are fastened on. In many instances, mirrors and legs are simply screwed on, in which case simply undo the screws, remove the part and then use woodfiller in the holes, sanding the surface smooth once it has dried. If the mirror or other unwanted section is attached with nails and glue, the problem is only slightly more difficult. Pry the surplus piece off, using a screwdriver or the claw side of a hammer, and then fill in any resulting holes with woodfiller. Extra sanding will probably be necessary as well, as the paint or varnish covering the piece will be raised above the newly bared surface. Tables can be lowered to coffee table or play table level simply by sawing off the legs to the desired height, measuring and marking carefully to make sure each leg matches the others and doesn't wobble by being either fractionally too long or too short. Sand smooth when finished.

Putting on: Most good do-it-yourself shops or wood suppliers have a standard stock of legs of various sizes. Simply choose the size and shape which best suits your need, and glue the new legs in position on all four corners of the chest using long, fine nails to secure them firmly.

Plain, flat-fronted chests or wardrobes (or even doors) can be ornamented in much the same way. Choose a standard moulding from a wood supplier and then—having measured each length carefully, mitring the corners if necessary—glue in place, using a few fine picture framing nails to secure them firmly. Fill any holes or gaps with woodfiller and sand smooth.

Reshaping Furniture 2
Below left: basic wooden bed, like those found in inexpensive hotels and second-hand shops all over the world.
Below right: the same bed with the footboard removed, given a pretty coat of paint and trompe l'oeil draperies 'tossed' over the head-board.

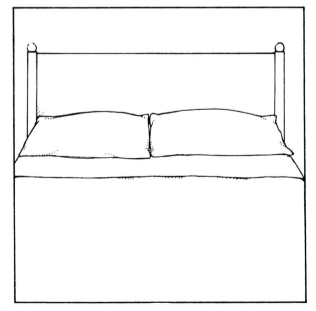

Simple Repairs

Broken or loose chair stretchers, rails or legs: Usually all that is needed is glue and firm clamping until the loose part is held tightly once again, but occasionally the damage is so severe that the piece will have to be replaced. This can be tricky, especially if the remaining stretchers or legs are carved, but woodstripping shops and suppliers specializing in stripped furniture often supply a spare parts service, with stray bits from otherwise unreclaimable furniture available for a small fee. Some will turn a new part for you, though obviously the price will be higher.

Broken or loose chair splats: Often you can find the top of the splat by looking for short dowels or sawn-off screws. If the splat is missing completely, chisel a small plug to fit from a bit of spare wood and glue in place, fitting the bottom first, and then sliding the top in position, well covered with glue.

Sticking drawers: Sticking is usually caused by dampness making the wood swell. Spread chalk on the drawer, close it, then open it. Where it has been rubbed away is where the drawer is sticking. Sand or plane away the extra wood. Seal with wax or oil to keep more moisture from entering and to help the drawer glide smoothly.

Split panels: Joints between panel sections can be reglued using temporary screws or pins at the back to hold them in place until the glue sets. Splits in the grain are trickier. If the crack is small, woodfiller can be used to cover the gap, sanded smooth once it is completely dry. If the crack is wide, the panel may have to be replaced.

Missing beading or moulding: Usually it is possible to find new moulding which matches fairly well. Most good wood suppliers or do-it-yourself shops have a wide range available. Always replace a complete section of moulding, not just the small portion which may have broken off. Clamp the new moulding firmly in place until the glue is dry.

Dents and deep scratches: These can be filled with woodfiller if they are deep enough; shallow hollows can be filled with an adhesive spackle, such as the new vinyl-based fine surface polyfillers. Sand smooth when the filler is completely dry.

Hinges: Often the only problem is worn screw holes. Use small hardwood plugs chipped off with a chisel from a small piece of wood, jamming them in firmly behind the screws and sanding

Below left: remove old screws from worn screw holes and insert small hardwood plugs.
Below centre: fill any cracks with woodfiller and sand smooth when dry.
Below right: replace the hinge, screwing into the new hardwood plugs.

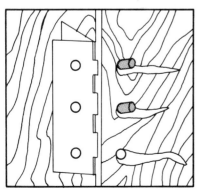
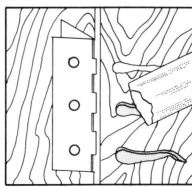
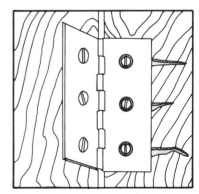

down any protruding edges with sandpaper.

Bubbles or broken veneer: If the veneer is in generally bad condition, you must remove it completely, sanding down the newly bared surface. If there is just a small bubble in the veneer, slit the centre of the bubble with a utility knife or razor blade, slip glue under the surface and press the veneer flat. A heavy book or other weight placed on top will help to hold the veneer flat until the glue dries thoroughly. Once the piece has been repaired, you can prepare it for painting.

If the piece is already painted, covered with varnish or French polished, you do not necessarily need to strip it down to the bare wood. If the existing finish is in good condition all you need to do is sand it smooth to make a good base for painting, taking particular care over any chips or breaks in the surface. If the paint or varnish is in poor condition, or was badly applied originally, you will have to strip it off, using any good proprietary paint stripper, following the brand instructions. Once the piece is stripped, it needs to be sanded smooth, using fine wire wool or sandpaper, rubbing always with the grain.

A small block of wood with the sandpaper wrapped around it is helpful, but in smaller areas your fingers will do. An electric sander can be useful for large, flat areas such as table tops, but beware of sanding discs fitted to electric drills which can form ugly grooves if you are inexperienced. A vacuum cleaner is the easiest way to clean up all the resulting dust.

The degree of time and care put into sanding depends on the degree of smoothness required for decorating successfully. If the piece is left in a solid colour, the surface should be extremely smooth, as any nicks and gauges show clearly.

The great advantage of decorative techniques, however, is that nearly all add to the surface texture and obscure any flaws which may be already there. The main exceptions are combing and any découpage which leaves large areas of the original surface bare.

Once the surface has been sanded as smoothly as required, and the resulting dust cleaned away, wipe down the piece with a cloth or sponge dipped in white spirit to take away any last trace of dust. From this point on, it is important to work cleanly, so spread fresh newspaper or plastic sheeting on the floor under your piece and prepare the paint and brushes.

Below left: a small plug is chiselled and inserted to secure a loose rail or leg.
Below centre: broken panels are secured with string laced around small nails and tightened, then glued.
Below right: missing bits of moulding are mitred to fit and glued in place.

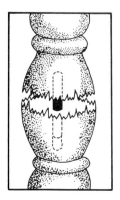
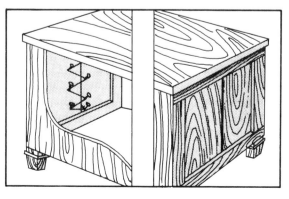
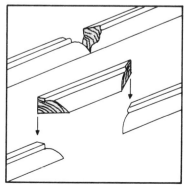

Painting the Base Coat

For the best paintwork, it is wise to invest in the best brushes you can afford. These are fat, with fine, silky bristles that hold a good amount of paint and spread it out at an even rate. Paint with straight even strokes, working always in the same direction. If you need to change direction, as, for example, in filling in around legs or mouldings, always finish with a light final stroke in the direction you have been brushing.

If the prepared surface is in a drastically different colour from the one you are about to work with, a first layer of undercoating gives good coverage and lessens the number of top coats you will have to add to get a pleasing depth of colour. Some of the newest paints have such thorough coverage however, that undercoating may not be necessary. The flower-stencilled table shown in the stencilling section of this book was painted with three coats of pale yellow eggshell oil-based paint directly over the original (well-sanded) polyurethaned pine. Ask your paint supplier for advice, if in doubt.

Always use a mid-sheen or eggshell or silk-finished oil-based paint for strength and durability. As soon as each coat of paint is thoroughly dry (allow at least 24 hours), rub it down gently with the finest grade of sandpaper. In this way you get rid of any bits of dust or hair that may have settled on the surface during drying and make a strong base for the next coat of paint. Wipe down with a cloth or sponge dipped in white spirits and allow to dry before painting the next layer.

With the second and later coats of paint, be as mean as you can while still covering the surface completely. In most cases three coats of paint (sanded between each) will be sufficient, but you may want to add a fourth coat wherever you expect extra wear, as on the tops of tables. When the last coat is dry, you are ready to begin decorating.

Special Problems

If you are working with man-made boards, in ready-made furniture or in a home-made table top, difficulties may arise in sanding and painting. The most common of these boards are plywood (made from several layers of veneer), blockboard (made from strips of softwood) and chipboard (made from wood particles bonded together with resin).

Both blockboard and plywood edges show end grain which absorbs paint to a greater degree than the rest of the wood and can produce rather a rough finish. If after priming the edges, you fill the rough grain with a proprietory interior plaster grade filler and rub it down smooth, when dry your finishing coats of paint will produce a smooth, even finish. Chipboard edges can be finished off with beaded moulding or can be prepared and painted in the same way as the edges of plywood and blockboard. As the abrasive quality of chipboard edges tend to tear ordinary sandpaper, steel-backed abrasive sheets, such as those supplied for hand sanders, may be easier to use. Also, the surface of the chipboard can profit from some fine filling before the paint will go on smoothly. Remember that bare blockboard or plywood, like all bare woods, must be primed before undercoating or painting.

Laminated cupboards can be painted reasonably well by carrying out the following procedure. First, wash down the cupboards thoroughly with hot water and detergent to remove every speck of dirt and grease. While they are wet, rub down with waterproof abrasive paper (320 grade). When the resulting slurry has been cleaned off and the surface is completely dry, brush on a coat of liquid alkyd gloss paint (*not* thixotropic or jellied) very thinly. Do not thin the paint with white spirit; spread thinly with the brush. When the first coat is dry, brush on one or two additional coats, rubbing down very lightly with the finest grade of wire wool before each. This should give a good base coat for decorating. A warning: this method is not advisable for laminated work tops, as no paint will adhere well enough to laminates to permit hard wear.

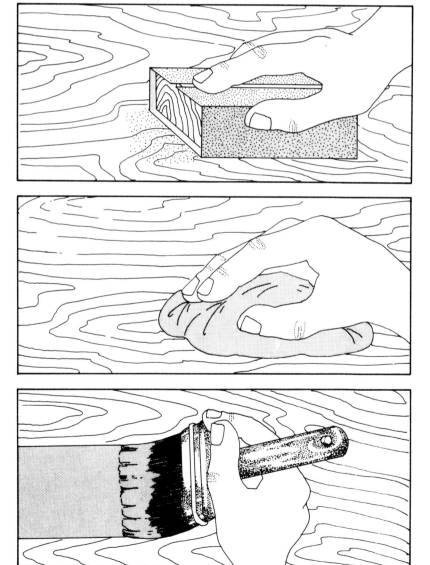

Top: rub down with fine sandpaper before beginning to paint and between each coat.
Centre: wipe with a cloth dipped in white spirit to remove dust.
Bottom: paint with straight smooth strokes, always moving in the same direction.

COLOUR

Colour is a magical tool which can transform the most miserable piece of furniture into a thing of beauty — and very cheaply too. It can make great objects seem smaller or give tiny, oddly shaped items importance. It can pull a batch of mismatched and separately acquired items into a customized set and turn dull sets of furniture into witty and original objets d'art. The same boring chest of drawers can be serious or funny, feminine or flamboyant, antiqued or futuristic, all depending on colour and how it is used.

Best of all, colour gives enormous freedom to the way in which furniture can be used. A brilliantly painted chest or table is like a bouquet of flowers, adding a colourful accent to a sober room. At the same time, an ugly but useful piece of furniture can be visually faded out with colour, disappearing almost completely when painted the same shade as the walls. A low table can become a learning tool for children, painted with all the names and colours of the rainbow, while a pair of ordinary second-hand office filing cabinets blossom, given a glossy coat of primary brights or more sophisticated shades, moving into a new life as toy storage, kitchen cabinets or even end tables in the sitting room. Colour sets the mood.

Colour also sets the period and the style. Any piece of furniture can be painted in the clear greens and yellows of Napoleonic France or the lush reds and blues of mid-Victorian England. Careful colouring places a piece in a particular style within a period of time. The colours of eighteenth-century London were quite unlike those of eighteenth-century Boston or New York, and those used by the elegant twenties' and thirties' decorator, Syrie Maugham, differed greatly from those used by her equally chic contemporary, Elsie de Wolfe. Museums keep careful records of colour usage in each period and a little research will provide whatever references you need.

Colour gives more than a sense of the period. Certain colours and colour combinations are delicate and romantic while others are gay and childlike, some are bizarre and others cheerily folkloric. The use of colour differs even within these categories. The colouring of Peruvian Indian folk art is quite unlike that of the Navajo Indian, while the subdued shades of Japanese peasant crafts are in contrast to the tropical brights of their Indonesian neighbours.

Greek houses are often painted wonderfully vibrant mixtures of cobalt blue and grass green or tangerine and turquoise while the heathery, greyed tones of the Scottish and English hills are repeated in the misty hues of traditional handknits and flowered chintz. Shades differ even within a fairly small area. The sprawling villages of Provence in France are coloured in rich, earthy terracottas and sands, while the towns of Bourgogne are more muted, bricks and gentle browns, violets and mauves.

Style, as expressed by colour, can be very specific. But it can be used merely to set a mood, mixing one style of colour with another style in form or decoration, creating a new look all your own. An eighteenth-century English patchwork pattern might be painted in sixteenth-century Japanese porcelain colours or a bouquet of tropical flowers — orchids, birds of paradise, lilies — may be stencilled in cool, wintry pales. The choice is up to you.

There is no correct way to use colour. The history of art is a history of artists deliberately and joyously breaking their predecessors' rules about how colour should be used. The point is to use the colours you love to give the effect you want. Professional artists and designers keep a constantly changing visual library of colour — clippings from magazines, scraps of fabric or yarn, postcards from museums and from trips abroad, books on art and on illustration, bits of embroidery — in fact everything and anything that catches their eye. Work out ideas in the same way, pinning a cutting of chintz next to an antique fan, laying out a patchwork quilt or Paisley shawl next to a book on Modern Art or Chinese porcelain.

Then experiment, playing with colour the way a child plays with crayons. A good selection of felt-tip pens or watercolours from an art supply shop gives you the basics, along with a plentiful supply of paper to work on. Lay bright colours next to bright, pale next to pale, and see how the colours work together. Try out the colours in your references — the blues and whites of porcelain, the muted red and browns of the Paisley shawl — and then add other accents, or small additions of colour, to the ones already there. Lay out little stripes or blocks of colour just for fun, striping pale grey with hot pink, or soft green with brick red. Then add third and fourth colours, both bright and pale, to see how the look changes.

Don't try to draw pictures with the colours. Apart from the little stripes and squares, keep the pattern abstract, for it is the play of colour with colour that is important at the moment, not the way it is used. Make dots or little circles, tiny dashes or crosses, or lay a wash of colour and dabble little spots all over the top. This is all good practice for the texturing techniques described later and also for hand painting.

Experiment with different intensities of colour, too. With four or five bottles of coloured drawing ink or diluted watercolour, lay stronger or more diluted layers of colour one over the other. Splatter thinned watercolour, drawing ink or even acrylic paints to give a wonderfully translucent effect; spatterings of thickened, almost creamlike colour give a different kind of intensity. Try a thinned wash of pale pink spattered or striped with thick, opaque red or a layer of opaque white dappled with thinned green and yellow.

Mixing colours properly takes practice, as well. While you

are playing with colour, let single drops of black fall one by one into the paint and see how the colour greys as a result. Do the same with blue and red, mixing tiny droplets into another colour and watching it change. The more you practice, the easier it will become to judge what is needed to bring a colour close to the shade you want. Although it is certainly safer and easier to work with existing colours—and there are excellent selections available in professional ranges of paint—there may be times when you want to match specific colours in a room or to satisfy your own creative impulse and knowing how to reach that colour will be important.

Decorative paint techniques soften the impact of flat, single colour. Cream overlaid with a glaze of greyed green is much gentler and softer than either cream or green on its own. Rich red glazed with black is at once richer and more muted than a coat of dark red would be. In the same way, a table spattered or marbled with green, blue and yellow over white and then edged with blue has a gentler look than the same table painted solid yellow or green and edged with the blue. Your colour palette is thus enlarged by the use of glazes and other decorative techniques.

Experiment to see how colours are altered by various techniques. It is always easier and more convenient to do this with a particular project in mind. When you are preparing to sponge or comb a painted piece of furniture, set aside time to play with the effect of differently coloured glazes on the piece before you actually begin. A few tablespoons of glaze can be coloured with various tints just for this purpose (see page 121 for details about glazes). Additional notes on experimenting are included in each section.

Traditional Colours

Traditional colours are, by their nature, reassuring and familiar. Soft blues and greens, reds and browns, honeys and creams can be put together in apparently random combinations to look as if they happened by chance over a period of years rather than by careful planning. Traditionals can be pale or dark, but what they have in common is a gentleness achieved both by the tones of the colours themselves, which are always rich and muted, and the way in which they are used. Medium blue, greyed with touches of black, a blued green also softened with drops of black, deep red dulled with blue and black, lightened by cream and accented with golden yellow and black is one combination seen in Victorian chintzes and early American folk art, in Oriental rugs and nineteenth-century porcelain. The intensity of the colours change, but the quality stays the same.

Contemporary decorators often work with colours which are not identified with any particular period, but which create a period effect; for example, dulled grey green accented with a line of gold or of deeper green, pale grey-blue softened with cream and possibly an edging of rose pink, or slightly greened yellow lined with gold and brown.

Antiqued Colours

Even softer than traditionals are 'antiqued' colours, apparently worn and dulled with age. Distressing or antiqueing is a technique which can vary from simple spatterings of black and brown or glazes which lay on an apparent coating of grime, to a complicated series of steps which try to duplicate the ravages of time.

Sponging, spattering and dragging are used to lay greyed or browned colour over another brighter or paler colour. Soft grey-blue can be sponged over white with spatterings of deeper grey, rose pink, burnt umber and sand, or soft green can be roughly spattered with brown and black, honey and blue. The more shades (and work) lavished on the antiqueing process, the softer and more beautiful the result.

Romantic Colour

When thinking of romance, the colour that comes quickest to mind is pink, the soft, gentle blush of old-fashioned roses. But that warm, heady glow comes with nearly all the colours of the garden, the rich pink of freesia, the golden yellow of daffodils, or the softer shades of wisteria and lilac, hyacinth and forget-me-not. Mixed with cream or white or paler tones of the same clear shades together with leafy greens, flower colours have buoyancy and charm. Use them all together in mixed bouquets straight from the garden or singly, as amusingly unexpected

A soft bouquet of painted leaves and flowers set on a latticework ground adds a romantic touch to any room.

accents in an otherwise sombre setting. Pop a glossy pink filing cabinet in the middle of a plain grey study or slip a wisteria table into a room that is predominantly soft green, or paint a vase of flowers onto a plain pine chest and place it in a clinically white setting.

Cheerful Colour

Fuschia pink, grass green, lollipop red, sunny yellow, sky blue—these are the colours children love best and the colours which add the most light and life to any room. Usually they are best handled in small doses and thus work wonderfully well applied to furniture. Use them all together, painting a wooden chair back yellow, the spokes blue, the seat red and the legs green, and switch the combination on other chairs in a set. A cherry red stool set in a plain white kitchen or bathroom, a sky blue table in a soft beige and brown room, or a chest painted happy stripes of fuchsia, white and yellow and placed in a pale pink bedroom are just a few ways to add youth and gaiety to an otherwise conventional setting.

Folkloric Colour

Naive or folk artists are by their nature untrained, untutored, and yet their direct and impassioned use of colour varies from the bright and childlike to the most sophisticated and subtle of combinations. Traditionally, their colours were limited to what was available from the land, natural dyes developed from insects and flowers, leaves and bark and from the earth itself. Indigos and browns, red and yellow ochres, blacks and creams, the most primitive of colours, were only altered when synthetic dyes became widely available. Even when that happened, certain peoples never changed, such as the Japanese and the Amerindians, but artists in the hot

Instant drama comes from painting a small table with bold Indian or Middle Eastern or African geometrics.

22

countries—India and Indonesia, Mexico and Peru—whose environment blazes naturally, embraced the new brights with delight and hot yellow and red, cobalt blue and brilliant green became as much a part of their folk art as the vegetable dyes which had come before. The bright colours spread to Middle Europe, as well, to Poland and Czechoslovakia, Russia and Rumania, moving north from the Mediterranean countries to whom brights were also a normal part of the scene.

There are thus two folk art palettes, both equally legitimate. One is composed of naturals—earth tones like sand and brown, red ochre and yellow ochre, black and indigo. The other is bright—the same primaries loved by children but much more intense—scarlet and violet, cobalt and emerald, sun yellow and hot pink.

The fiery heat of these colours—for even the earth tones glow—adds richness and vigour to any room. Use them together—indigo and yellow ochre, cobalt and black—or separately, painting a pair of director's chairs hot pink and cutting the back and seat in emerald green, or covering the top of a table in the intricate geometric of a Cree Indian's porcupine quill shirt, all in soft red ochre paired with cream and black.

Experimental Colour

This is colour at its most innovative and extreme. The colours of avant garde fashion are here, along with the work of the Post Modernist movement in art and design. Most often, these are the colours of the future, but as always in creative thinking, whether in art or design or fashion or films, the most forward looking experiments are the most difficult for the average viewer to accept and appreciate.

But it is always worth looking, for it is only with time that the new becomes the familiar. Pastels make an easy example. It has taken more than eight years for the soft pinks and greens, blues and greys which are now offered to the average consumer at minimal cost to reach this degree of acceptability. When they first appeared in the work of interior designers such as Tricia Guild of Designer's Guild, they appealed mainly to a small and very sophisticated market. Now they are everywhere, and a new palette for interiors is being explored by the avant garde.

Decorated furniture makes an ideal testing ground for experimental colour. The expense is small and if you hate the result you can paint it out and start again. Look at new painting, new design and try out the colours for yourself, black paired with pale pink and blue, or chartreuse mated with cobalt and mauve. Research into the past may provide material for the future as designers find new inspiration in the work of the Arts and Crafts movement or the furniture of the Fifties, in the Cubists' interest in African art or the Surrealists' joy in the unexpected. You could zebra stripe a chest in hot pink and black or fling a kaleidoscope of colour over a chair. All it takes is imagination and a little time.

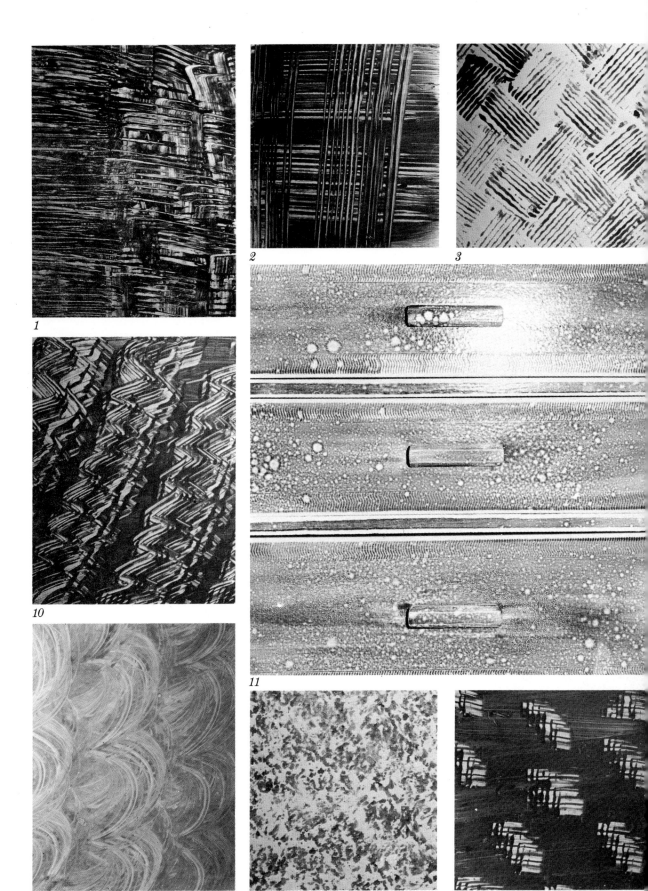

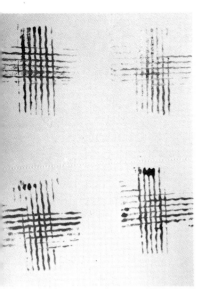

TECHNIQUES

Introducing Texture

Giving a textured finish to a piece of furniture is no more difficult than baking a cake. There are a set of simple rules to follow and provided they are followed carefully, little can go wrong. The look of the textured surface can be varied endlessly by changing the materials or method of applying them just a little bit. All it takes is courage and patience and a willingness to experiment and learn.

Basically, there are two ways of creating texture. Colour can be applied to a plain, painted surface with a tool, such as a sponge or brush or bit of crumpled newspaper, which gives the paint or glaze an irregular texture. Alternatively, paint or glaze can be brushed onto a plain, painted surface and then partially removed while wet with a tool, such as a sponge or brush or bit of crumpled newspaper, leaving a textured pattern behind. Complicated, highly sophisticated textures are created by combining these methods.

In the following pages, many ways of applying and removing colour will be explained, but these are meant to be guidelines only. Once you have practised and mastered each of the basic techniques, you will be ready to create new combinations and methods of your own.

Painted textured finishes are as numerous and varied as the people who create them. Each style has a different appeal. Early American naive painted furniture delights by its vigour and simplicity, while much contemporary painted furniture pleases by quiet understatement. Either of these effects can be achieved with colour and texture applied with the simplest of tools. All it takes is a little experimentation to discover what works best for you.

Quick, loose strokes with a bit of sea sponge or plastic scrubbing pad or any other similar rough tool give a variety of textures which can be dramatic and bold or soft and pretty depending on the colours used. Squares of ridged cardboard draw sharply marked criss-crosses in wet glaze (1) or free-flowing plaids (2) or a series of overlapping L shapes, either covering the surface (3) or spaced out (7). The same piece of cardboard makes marvellous zig-zagging stripes (10), or, dipped lightly into paint and used as a stamp, marks crisp, neat crosses (4) or a latticework (6). A square of plastic scrubbing pad scribbles overlapping circles (5) or half-moons (9) in the wet glaze or, dipped into paint and squeezed almost dry, can be used to sponge on its own allover texture (8). Easiest of all, the starry and sophisticated effect achieved by spattering white spirits onto the wet paint or glaze (11).

Sponging and Pouncing On

The speediest way to add colour and texture to a plain painted chest or table is to sponge it on, that is, to dip a piece of coarse natural sponge into some thinned paint or glaze and dab it onto the surface. The effect depends on the number and translucency of the colours sponged on, one over the other, and the type of applicator used.

Even at its most basic, this technique can work wonders. Cheap white enamelled kitchen cabinets melt softly into the background when sponged lightly with the same colour as the kitchen walls. With more time and care, a gentle build-up of delicately tinted glazes can give a faux marble look to a plain chipboard table.

The colour and transparency of the paint are the key factors. Opaque colour, such as paint used straight from its container, is the most dramatic, especially when used in strongly contrasting shades. Tinted glazes or thinned oil paints give subtlety and a lovely translucent look which is softer and more sophisticated.

The surface texture varies with the tool used for dabbing on the paint. A variety of tools can be used to lay on the colour, each giving a special look and pattern of its own.

Materials: A natural, marine sponge (artificial sponges cannot be substituted as the holes are too regular to give a satisfactory result); coarse wire wool, or a kitchen pan scrubber; crumpled paper or a plastic bag squeezed into a ball; a piece of flexible or rigid cardboard; glaze or thinned oil paint; tinters or artists' oil paints; white spirit; 3in (75mm) brush for painting on the glaze; shallow dish or dishes, one for each colour; rags or paper towelling for cleaning up.

Before beginning: Prepare the piece for decorating as described on pages 10–17. Mix colours (see page 121).

Method: Put a small amount of coloured glaze or oil-based paint in a shallow dish and thin it slightly with a few drops of white spirit. Wearing gloves, if desired, dip the sponge lightly into the thinned paint or glaze and squeeze it to shed any excess. Test quickly on a piece of waste paper to make sure the sponge is not overloaded and then dab it gently but firmly onto the surface to be textured. Repeat, working with a light dabbing motion until the area is covered in a cloudy colour. When the first layer of glaze is completely dry, sponge on a second, slightly overlapping the first colour to give a dappled effect. A third (or fourth) colour can be applied in the same way. Change the way the sponge is held (or cloth or scrubbing pad) from time to time to give variety to the texture. It is important to clean the sponge frequently, squeezing it out thoroughly in white spirit, (or take a new piece of paper or plastic bag if that is your sponging tool), whenever the impression begins to smudge.

Sponging with two or more colours creates a balanced effect. If one colour begins to dominate, a few dabs of the second colour, or even of the base colour, tones it down. Highlights and accents may be added at the end in the same way.

Different effects can be achieved by cutting the applicator into shapes—squares, triangles, circles,—and sponging on the paint in a predetermined pattern. When the finished piece is completely dry—and this can take a week or more in damp weather—protect it with two or more coats of polyurethane varnish, sanding down between each coat.

Pouncing On

This is the same as sponging on, but a small stiff brush is used to lay on the colour in a springy, almost bouncing movement. The brush is held high up on the handle, perpendicular to the surface, then dabbed onto the surface lightly but firmly enough to spread the bristles a little with each pounce. The brush is moved back and forth over the area already covered to texture it evenly.

As in sponging, the brush is dipped into the paint and tapped out on waste paper. When the touch of the brush leaves a soft, even tone, it is ready. Pat the brush up and down so that it almost bounces with each stroke. Each time the brush is dipped into the paint, test it out on clean paper before pouncing.

It is best to begin at the edges of a piece, with a freshly loaded brush, and work towards the middle as the colour lightens. To highlight carvings and mouldings, wipe gently with a soft, clean cloth as soon as the pouncing is complete.

Pouncing gives the finest, most delicate texture of all the techniques. For a soft antique look, darkened shades of thinned oil-based paint or glaze are pounced over pale or vivid colours to mute them slightly. A denim blue pounced over clear sky blue or black over bright red are obvious choices, but a gentle rose could be successfully pounced over pale pink, or a deep caramel over yellow.

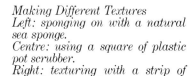

Making Different Textures
Left: sponging on with a natural sea sponge.
Centre: using a square of plastic pot scrubber.
Right: texturing with a strip of ridged cardboard.

Spattering

Early American colonials, unable to afford rugs, often painted their floors in a mixture of colours, spattered and swirled in gay abandon—or so it seemed. In fact, the paint was quite tightly controlled; the choice of colour and the delicacy or coarseness of the spray determined whether the effect was elegant or naive. Sometimes the spattered effect was used as a background for hand-painted or stencilled rugs, apparently scattered on the floor.

This technique can also be used for furniture, spattering a mixture of colours over a base coat and framing the effect with a fine line of colour or with a stencilled or hand-painted border—or even with a *trompe l'oeil* mat painted or stencilled in the centre of a chest or table.

The technique is extremely simple. A small, stiff brush—an old toothbrush is ideal—is dipped into slightly thinned paint and then tapped with a short stick (or an old table knife) so that a spray of paint falls onto the surface to be decorated. The only skill to be mastered is controlling the amount of paint that falls from the brush at each tap.

A single colour spattered over a contrasting base can be charming by itself—a soft blue or rose pink spattered over cream gives a pretty, gentle look similar to that of Portuguese pottery sprayed with pink or blue glaze over cream and then fired to a high sheen. A crisp, leafy green over white is fresh and clean, while three or more colours spattered lightly over each other can give an effect roughly resembling marble. The faux marble look is especially strong when the colours are close in tone—shades of beige or grey over cream, for example, possibly highlighted with muted blue or green.

Streaks or swirls of colour were often dashed over the spatter on colonial American floors, and can be charming on coarsely spattered tables. Again, the technique is simple. A small, cotton-tipped stick—those sold for cosmetic use are ideal—is dipped in paint straight from the container (here, the thickness and slight viscous quality is important) and then flicked over the surface with a quick twist of the wrist.

Spattering is used to give an aged or antique look to many painted finishes, and for this a much finer spray is needed. This is achieved by dipping the toothbrush in the thinned paint and, having tapped off any excess, running a finger lightly over the bristles to produce a fine shower of colour.

Colours for antiqueing are generally dark—brown or black—to give the look of dirt deposited on the surface over many years. The spatter should not be too even, as it looks more natural if the colour is denser in some areas than in others.

For a delicately freckled look, India ink is used, diluted

Drop Spattering
A light spattering of paint falls when the toothbrush is tapped gently.

slightly with water so that mistakes can be wiped away. The technique here is slightly different in that only a few bristles of the brush are flicked to keep the spray really sparse. If the speckling is too heavy, it can be wiped away and flicked on again. After the ink is dry, any surplus spatters can be rubbed out with the finest grade of wire wool. The same fine wire wool can be used to soften the all-over effect when the ink is dry.

Fine spatters of a single colour, as for antiqueing, can be treated in a number of ways. For instance, the spattered surface is brushed lightly and diagonally across the grain in both directions with a small, stiff brush or toothbrush just before the paint has dried. This gives a gentle, slightly blurred look. Alternatively, when the spatter is about half dry, it is followed by a spatter of white spirits. This dissolves the spatter slightly, producing a softened effect. The dissolution can be controlled by patting the surface delicately with fine wire wool or a soft, clean pad of muslin.

Materials: An old toothbrush (one for each colour to be used); an old table knife; cotton-tipped sticks; mid-sheen oil-based paint; white spirit; small glass jars or bowls (again, one for each colour); newspapers or polythene sheeting to protect the floor; rags or paper towelling for cleaning up. Rubber kitchen gloves to keep paint off your hands are a good extra. If you are spattering a large piece, such as a wardrobe, a small paint brush, cut off about 1in (25mm) from the handle and used in place of the toothbrush, will help the work go more quickly.

Before beginning: Prepare the piece of furniture for decorating as described on pages 10 — 17. Put a few spoonfuls of each colour of paint (mixed as described on page 121) in its own jar and thin slightly with white spirit. The paint should be about the consistency of light cream.

Method: The area which is to be spattered must always be horizontal, otherwise the blobs of paint will run. This means that the piece of furniture to be decorated may have to be turned on its side or back. Once the piece is in position, begin by dipping the toothbrush into the first colour and tapping it once or twice with the table knife to knock off excess paint. Then, holding the toothbrush over the surface to be spattered, tap the brush repeatedly with the knife, moving it slowly over the area until the brush is dry. Repeat until the area is completely flecked with colour, in a soft, cloudy effect.

The second and third colours can be spattered on over the first while it is still wet; slight bleeding of one colour into another really doesn't matter. The wet surface must not be moved, however, until the droplets of paint are dry to the touch. Turning will make the spattering run.

Generally, anything which is spattered takes far longer to dry than any other technique; the blobs of paint are thick and stay soft often for a week or more. The advantage of this slow drying, however, is that any really large blobs of paint can be scraped away carefully with the point of a razor bade while the paint is still pliable. Final finishing with polyurethane varnish must wait until the entire surface has dried hard.

Streak Spattering
Streaks result when a cotton-tipped stick, dipped in paint is tapped.

Colourwashing, Dry Brushing and Dragging

Colourwashing gives a delicate, watery shadow of colour, softening the harshness of a plain colour and lending it depth. The technique is simple; a coat of much thinned oil-based paint is brushed over an eggshell base. A sunny yellow washed over white gives a lovely glowing look, far prettier than plain yellow paint, while a soft caramel washed over pale sandy grey gives a gentle, antiqued finish.

Colourwashing can be used as a base for more ambitious effects as well. A chest colourwashed in bright red over white can then be spattered with black and white, or it might be colourwashed in a soft green over pale grey and then sponged with a deep watery blue. More ambitious is the table colourwashed with rosy pink blurred into sky blue with sponged-on clouds of white. Colourwashing makes a pretty background for stencilling, too.

Materials: Flat oil-based paint; white spirit; a 3in (75mm) brush; a large bowl or pan in which to put the colourwash; plenty of clean rags or paper towelling for cleaning; and lots of newspaper or polythene sheeting to protect the floor. Watered down gouache or acrylic paints could be used as alternatives to the flat oil-based paint.

Before beginning: Prepare the piece for decorating as described on pages 10—17, and mix colours, if necessary, as explained on page 121.

Thin the colour drastically with white spirits, aiming for a clear, watery look when tested on waste paper.

Method: Dip the brush into the wash and paint the colour on loosely all over the surface, going over it to avoid brushmarks and hard edges. Leave some untouched areas and then, when the wash is dry, repeat, brushing over the plain areas and over most of the already coloured areas to leave an attractive irregularity of colour.

Thinned paint will dry quickly, but it is best to let each coat dry overnight, otherwise you will find that you are taking colour off the second time around, rather than putting more on. Don't worry if it all seems to run the first time you brush it on, you may have to spread the paint around a bit to make it take, especially on the vertical bits of your chest or table. The first coat may also look quite patchy, but this does not matter; the second coat will pull it altogether in a glowing finish.

When the wash is completely dry, finish with two or more coats of polyurethane varnish, sanding down between each coat, as always.

Dry Brushing

The opposite of colourwashing is dry brushing. As its name

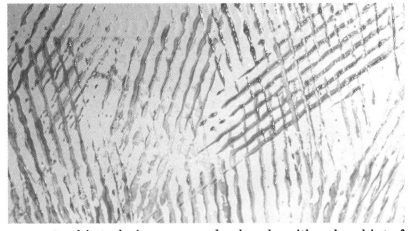

Dry brushing in closely related shades gives a soft, antiqued effect.

suggests, this technique uses a dry brush, with only a hint of colour on it, to lay on a light, random texture. But where colourwashing is nearly always delicate, dry brushing can be bold or soft, depending on the colour and the strength of the strokes.

Dry brushing can be used very simply on its own, such as the striking kitchen in which the cabinets and walls were dry brushed in bold, cross-hatched strokes of white on clear blue. More often it is used over other techniques, such as sponging or rag rolling, to add extra colour and a change in texture. A single colour or several colours may be dry brushed on, depending on the desired result. Dry brushing is particularly effective on the inset panels of a chest or wardrobe, as part of the overall design.

Materials: Ordinary clean, dry brushes of varying widths, depending on the type of effect required; mid-sheen finish, oil-based paint; white spirit; rags or paper towelling for cleaning; polythene sheeting or newspaper to protect the floor.

Before beginning: The piece is prepared for decorating, as described on pages 10—17, or decorated with colourwashing, sponging, rag rolling, or any of the other basic texturing finishes.

Method: Dip the brush lightly into the paint and wipe most of it away on newspaper. When only a hint of colour is left, brush it on quickly in a series of light, swift strokes crossing each other in a random manner.

When the paint is completely dry, finish with two or more coats of polyurethane varnish, sanding down between each coat, as always.

Dragging

This technique is what its name implies. A light coat of glaze is applied with a brush onto a painted surface and then a second, clean brush is pulled or dragged through the wet colour, pulling off strips of glaze so that the base colour shows through. The effect is subtle and somewhat formal and has ornamented luxurious homes since the thirties when it was popularized by interior decorators such as Elsie de Wolfe and Syrie Maugham.

Usually the colours are soft—sludge grey dragged over dull green, rich honey over cream—in order to create a muted, slightly antique look. More dramatic colours can be spectacular, however, with combinations like burnt orange dragged over pearl grey, or black over emerald, turning an unexceptional piece of furniture into a showpiece.

Other tools can be used for dragging, too, such as the coarsest grade of wire wool or a plastic mesh scrubbing pad, even a rolled up plastic mesh bag, each giving a slightly different type of striation.

The dragged surface itself can be treated in various ways. While the glaze is still wet it can be softened and blended with a pad of muslin or a piece of sponge. When the colour is dry it can be rubbed lightly with the finest grade of wire wool to highlight mouldings or carving, or simply to make the striated colour even more irregular. It combines very well with other techniques, for instance spattering is often used over dragged surfaces, both to enhance the feeling of age and to add extra colour and texture.

Materials: Oil-based, mid-sheen paint thinned to transparency, or transparent oil glaze tinted to the colour desired (see page 121 for details); two 4in (100mm) brushes; a paint tray or shallow pan; white spirit; lots of rags or paper towelling for cleaning; polythene sheeting or newspaper to protect the floor.

Dragging brushes with extra long, flexible bristles for stronger lines can be bought, but these are expensive. However, if you are going to do a lot of dragging, they are probably worth looking for in a specialist paint store or trade suppliers.

Before beginning: Prepare your piece for decorating as described on pages 10—17. For dragging, it is important to make sure the surface is free from nicks and small holes, as they will show up in the decorated finish. Preliminary filling and sanding are more important with dragging than with many of the other textures which, by their nature, tend to hide imperfections.

Method: Brush on an even coat of glaze, starting from the top of the area to be textured taking it straight to the bottom. It is helpful to start where a natural line already exists, such as the edge of a chest or table. Then take the dry brush and firmly, but lightly, pull it down through the wet band of glaze. Repeat, cleaning the dragging brush every few strokes to make sure it continues to take paint off instead of putting it on. Do not worry about keeping the lines absolutely straight; a slight wobble is to be expected and will not be noticed when the piece is finished and in place.

When the glaze is completely dry, protect with two or more coats of polyurethane varnish, sanding down between each coat.

Professional decorators sometimes spatter the wet glaze lightly with colour before dragging, adding bright or soft accents to the overall texture.

This set of second-hand chairs was painted white and then sponged with pink before being recovered in pink silk brocade for the private dining room of an elegant London restaurant.

Pouncing, Sponging Off, Stippling and Vinegar Painting

In pouncing or sponging off, a layer of glaze is brushed lightly over a plain painted surface and immediately partially removed, using a brush or sponge or wad of newspaper or even tips of your fingers, leaving a soft pattern or texture behind. Nothing could be simpler; and yet, depending on the tool and the way that it is used, an almost endless variety of decorative effects can be achieved.

That lightly glazed surface can be pounced or dabbed at with a ball of crumpled plastic or muslin or a piece of coarse wire wool, a plastic pot scrubber or an old wine bottle cork, an old nail brush or the palm of your hand. It can be scraped with a roughly cut comb (for more on combing, see pages 51—52), a piece of ridged cardboard, a fork or fingernails. It can be stroked with a feather or rolled with a bit of clean rag, an old terry towel—or even a wad of newspaper.

In short, you can use anything and do almost anything that achieves a pleasing effect. And if you don't like the look of what you've done, you can wipe it away and start again.

The point is to experiment. Start with a small bit of painted wood—the drawer of a chest, the top of a little table or just a piece of chipboard. Brush on the glaze or thinned oil-based paint, and play, wiping each test pattern off as you finish and starting again. When you've found a pattern or combination of effects that you like, you are ready to begin decorating a real piece of furniture.

Materials: Oil-based, mid-sheen paint thinned to transparency or transparent oil glaze tinted to the colour desired (as explained on page 121); white spirit; clean rags or paper towelling for cleaning up; and any of the following tools: for pouncing—a small, stiff brush with the bristles cut off to about 1in (25mm) from the handle (a large stencilling brush is an acceptable substitute) or a natural marine sponge; for stippling— a plastic pot scrubber, a piece of ridged cardboard, newspaper, plastic bags, old terry towelling, or muslin.

Before beginning: Prepare the piece for decorating as described on pages 10—17.

Method: The technique for pouncing, stippling and sponging is exactly the same; it is the texture which differs. Stippling is the word used for texturing with a brush or a small pad; pouncing is much the same, except the brush or pad is pressed harder into the glaze; sponging is again the same, using a sponge or other soft fabric. In each case, the tool is dabbed or patted into the wet glaze, creating an all-over texture with no gaps or hard edges. At all times, it is important to clean your brush or sponge frequently to make sure you are removing paint and not simply blurring it.

If you are using a ball of crumpled newspaper or plastic, or fabric, crumple it tightly into a wad small enough to hold in your fingertips and turn it frequently to make sure you keep a fairly clean area for texturing. When the material is soaked and is no longer able to remove paint, it is time to replace it with a fresh piece.

Ridged cardboard can be used to make more defined patterns if it is cut into shapes such as squares or triangles. A square of corrugated board makes a marvellous checkerboard pattern, used carefully.

Finally, if you are using the tips of your fingers to pounce, remember to clean them frequently, just like any other tool, to keep the impression crisp and clear.

Ragging and Rolling

Ragging is just a variation of sponging. For this a piece of fabric such as old shirting, terry towelling, or a plastic shopping bag, is made into a wad, and held in one hand. It is pressed firmly and gently into the paint, lifted, turned slightly and pressed again. This process is repeated quickly and loosely all over the surface to be textured and gives a lovely, soft crumpled texture which is subtle and very pleasing.

Rolling uses crumpled fabric or plastic, or even wads of newspaper, but this time the wadding is loose and open and rolled across the wet glaze, just like turning a rolling pin over pastry. The effect is more open than in ragging, giving a texture not unlike that of antique leather. Once again, it is important to keep the fabric clean, replacing it with a fresh ball as soon as it is soaked with paint.

Professional decorators often spatter bits of colour into the wet glaze before ragging or rolling it. Alternatively, sections can be ragged or rolled in slightly different colours, occasionally overlapping for a lovely cloudy effect.

Vinegar Painting

An exuberant variation of all these texturing techniques is vinegar painting—a brash, lighthearted medium used instead of ordinary paint. Where glazes and thinned oil paints produce subtle and sophisticated textures, the vinegar mix (vinegar, sugar, powder paint and dishwashing detergent) takes a bold impression of anything that is pressed onto it: a wine bottle cork, a blob of plasticine, a scrap of crumpled paper—the coarser the tool, the freer and more adventurous the patterns made with it.

Materials: Paint medium—sugar, dishwashing detergent, artists' or children's powder paints; empty glass jars for mixing. For texturing—wine bottle corks, plasticine, window putty, crumpled aluminium foil or newspaper; plus plenty of rags and paper towelling for cleaning.

Method: Put three or four heaped tablespoons of the powder paint into one glass jar. In the other put about half a cup of vinegar, a heaped spoon of sugar and a good squeeze of detergent; mix the three together thoroughly and then put a spoonful into the powder paint. Mix to a smooth paste. Add the rest of the vinegar solution and mix it all together well. Dab a bit on some paper and hold it up vertically. If the solution runs, it is too thin. Put a little more powder into the first jar and mix again as described.

Take the time to become accustomed to this new technique before beginning to work on a piece of furniture. Brush on the solution and experiment, dabbing each of your texturing tools in turn until you feel confident you understand the difference between using the vinegar medium and using glazes. Then begin. Among the advantages of vinegar painting is its brilliance of colour, due to the use of pure pigment.

Finish with two or more coats of varnish, sanding down between each coat, as always.

This old kitchen table was shortened to coffee table height and painted white, then spattered with yellow, blue and green. Blue lines frame the top and sides to give a crisp finish.

Rich blue sponging (left) transforms this basic white kitchen.

Cream and honey marbelizes the top of an old washstand (below) in a restaurant ladies' room. Dragging and wiping in the same colours softened the carving below. The mirror just above, a junk shop find, was sponged with shades of blue to match the wallpaper.

Rolled and Pounced Desk

This junk shop desk was transformed with old rags and newspaper, a used wine bottle cork, some masking tape and two colours of paint. These, plus a sharp set of fingernails, were all that was needed to produce several different decorative textures—each quick and easy to learn—which were put together to turn this sow's ear into a piece of elegance and charm.

The main techniques—pouncing and rolling—were combined with wiping (or cleaning the glaze away to create highlights) and combing (see pages 51—52), to show how several patterns and textures can be used together in apparently complicated effects.

Planning

To begin with, the desk was covered with battered white paint and missing part of one leg. Basically elegant and traditional in shape, it fitted the Victorian setting intended for it, but needed a finish which would hide its flaws. Pouncing in a dark colour was the answer; the rough texture would hide nicks and irregularities in the surface and the deep shade would mask

Below left: brushing on the glaze.
Below centre; pouncing with a ball of crumpled newspaper.
Below right; scratching the wiggly border with fingernail tips.

them. There were several possible choices: tobacco brown over yellow ochre, cocoa over soft blue, or black over emerald green. The decision was eminently Victorian, black over bright red, with the dark glaze deepening the red to a rich glow.

The same piece could have been moved to a lighter setting, as a dressing table in a bedroom or bathroom, for example, simply by switching the colours. A strong cobalt blue pounced over white or café au lait over peach would have changed the mood of the desk completely.

Materials: Mid-sheen oil-based paint, or glaze; tinters or artists' oil paints in the colours required; old newspaper; a wine bottle cork; 2in (50mm) masking tape; white spirit; lots of clean rags.

Method: The desk was prepared for decoration as described on pages 10—17. When the final coat of bright red had dried thoroughly (allowing at least 24 hours), a light coat of black glaze was brushed onto the centre of the side panel. Immediately, while the glaze was still wet, a sheet of newspaper was crumpled into a ball, small enough to hold firmly in one hand, and dabbed or pounced over the surface until the area was textured.

The raised panels at either end of the side panel were then brushed with glaze and, using three fingernails on one hand, a light wavy stroke was scratched down through the wet glaze. When the edges were wiped, using a clean rag dampened with white spirit and wrapped tightly around one finger, the side panel was complete. The same techniques were repeated on the other side and also on the back panel of the desk.

The top of the desk, which is on view most of the time, presented the greatest challenge. It was masked in sections and two different techniques separated by a third were used to create the effect of a leather-topped surface, in keeping with the nineteenth-century look. Although this sounds complicated, it was, in fact, quite straightforward.

The top was large enough to allow three generous borders around the centre panel. Two main textures alternated, with the third dividing the two and adding strength and variety.

Below left: wiping the edge clean with a cloth dampened with white spirit and wrapped tightly around the forefinger.
Below centre; a border of overlapping fingermarks is tested.
Below right: it is rejected in favour of a simple stripe drawn with an old wine-bottle cork.

The centre panel was masked off first, using 2 in (50mm) masking tape, positioned with careful measuring to keep the lines straight, to make a 4x29in (100x725mm) panel. The middle border, which would repeat the same texture, was masked off at the same time, with a 2½in (62mm) gap left between the two masked-off areas and also between the middle border and the edge of the desk for the first and third borders which would be added later.

The centre panel was then brushed with glaze and rolled in the following way: a sheet of old newspaper was crumpled loosely (less tightly than for pouncing) and rolled over, slowly and firmly, in the wet glaze until the surface was textured. The same process was repeated in the masked-off border, using a fresh sheet of newspaper. The resulting effect looked not unlike leather. When the glaze was dry to the touch (usually after twenty-four hours) the masking tape was removed.

The plain borders were brushed with glaze, slightly overlapping the already decorated edges, and then patterned with the same wavy fingernail stroke as used on the sides.

While the glaze was still wet, the lines between the two textures were sharpened by drawing a thick line with the cork. This was done by running the cork firmly and swiftly through the wet glaze.

To finish off the top, the ridged mouldings framing the surface were brushed with glaze and wiped to bring them into relief.

The front of the drawers and their casings were pounced, using the same technique as on the sides, with each drawer framed with a thick line drawn by the cork. To give a crisp, neat finish, the drawer casings had their edges wiped as well, and the wavy fingernail stroke used on the sides and top was repeated on the raised panels on each side of the front of the desk. Finally, the legs were pounced to complete the gentle, muted effect.

The glaze was left to dry for a week to make sure it was hard, then covered with two coats of mid-sheen polyurethane varnish, sanded lightly between coats. Finally, a piece of bevelled glass was cut to fit and protect the top from wear.

Below left: the glaze is brushed onto the masked-off centre panel.
Below centre: holding the crumpled newspaper tightly in both hands, roll it over and over in the wet glaze.
Below right: a strong band edging the panel is drawn with a firm stroke using an old wine-bottle cork.

Left: the rich interplay of pattern is delightful.
Below: the completed desk seen in its final setting. The same techniques applied in caramel on cream would give a much softer mood, preferable in a paler setting. Alternatively hot pink on baby pink would turn this into a charming dressing table for a very feminine bedroom or bathroom.

Peacock Feather Chest

An absurdly simple, whimsical effect can be produced by brushing on a coat of glaze and then dotting it like the eye of a peacock's feather with the inner knuckle of one hand. The body of this little chest was patterned in just this way. But then, in the manner of naive or folk artists, a second pattern was added to the first—a combed woodgrain which is only slightly more difficult to achieve than the peacock's eye.

Either technique would be charming used all over this little piece. Depending on colour, the effect can be sophisticated or rustic. In deep, brick red brushed and dotted over black, the chest would slip neatly into a simple country cottage. In soft sand, brushed and patterned with tobacco, it would sit easily in a contemporary town house. The wilder and more dramatic the colours, for instance, black over magenta or emerald, the wittier the completed piece.

Materials for the peacock's feather: Glaze or thinned oil-based paint; white spirit; plenty of rags or paper towelling for cleaning; a brush for laying on the glaze.

Before beginning: Prepare for decorating as described on page 11. Mix coloured glaze or thinned oil-based paint.

Method: Brush on a fairly even amount of glaze. Immediately, holding the right hand stiffly, with all of the fingers arched back as far as they will go, take the index finger in the left hand and press it back as far as it will go comfortably. This will make the palm-side cushion of the knuckle stand out.

Press this cushion against the wet glaze quickly and firmly, in a random, spaced out pattern, filling in dots until the design is pleasing. Repeat, until the entire surface is dotted.

Materials for the combed woodgrain: For the comb—a piece of fairly stiff plastic, such as the side of a plastic bottle

Note: there is a section on comb painting, beginning on page 50 with specific instructions for making combs.

Below left: the hand arched in position, with the index finger pulled back using the other hand.
Centre: the surface is dotted with the palm side of the knuckle.
Right: a meandering accent line is drawn with the home-made comb to mark the woodgrain.

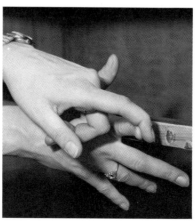
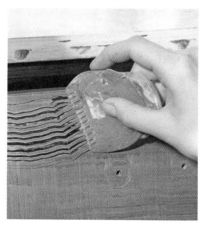

containing white spirit or fabric softener, or the plastic lid of a tin. Using scissors, cut a rectangle approximately 4 x 3 in (100mm x 75mm). On the wider edge, cut randomly shaped teeth of varying widths, from narrow to fairly wide. This is your woodgraining comb.

A fine camel's hair brush; glaze or thinned oil-based paints; tinters; a brush to lay on the glaze; 2 — 3 in (50 — 75mm) brush for texturing; rags or paper towelling for cleaning.

Method: Brush on a light, smooth coat of glaze. Holding the comb firmly in one hand, run it slowly and irregularly through the wet colour, starting at one corner of the area to be textured. Move the comb in a random, wavy stroke to imitate the meandering, slightly jagged pattern of real woodgrain. Repeat, making a second band of graining next to and slightly overlapping the first. Continue working with the comb until the area is completely textured.

Immediately, take the clean, dry brush and smudge some of the lines slightly by drawing the brush quickly and lightly through the still wet glaze in a series of short, parallel strokes angled across the bands of graining. The touch of the brush should be fast and very delicate. The aim is to mute the lines a little, just as lines of real woodgrain are sometimes softened.

A few more definite, bolder lines of graining enhance the realistic effect. To make them, the plastic graining comb is folded over to form a tight U-shape and it is this which is used as the graining tool. Holding the folded comb tightly in the fingers, draw the U-edge through the wet glaze in a loose, wandering line which follows the graining already drawn. Repeat a few inches away. Only an occasional accent line is needed — perhaps two on the average drawer — as they are meant to highlight the texture only, not dominate it.

Finally, a few light, squiggly lines are painted on top of the graining with the fine, camel's hair brush. To make them, dip the brush in the glaze and, very delicately, paint a series of loose, slightly wavy parallel lines in groups of half-a-dozen or more across the lines of graining, in the same direction as the dry brush strokes made earlier. These clusters of little lines should vary in width, tapering at the beginning or the end of

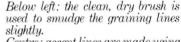

Below left: the clean, dry brush is used to smudge the graining lines slightly.
Centre: accent lines are made using the comb folded into a U shape.
Right: a few squiggly lines are drawn across the grain using an artists' brush.

each group. Once again, they imitate natural wood, and a certain amount of roughness and irregularity is important.

In woodgraining a chest of drawers, it is important to work while the drawers are in place, but opened slightly, to avoid painting the frame. The pattern of the graining must be

The mix of combed woodgrain and dotting gives an artless, naive look which is very charming. More vivid colours, such as fuchsia and scarlet, for example, would move this same piece into a bolder, contemporary setting while the quieter shades of, say, chocolate and sand would give it a more masculine feel.

planned considering the piece as a whole, balancing the lines and highlights with a view to the overall effect.

When the glaze is completely dry (a week or more in damp climates) protect the finish with two or more coats of polyurethane varnish, sanding down between each coat.

Delicate and Bold Woodgrains

Delicate Woodgrain

To paint delicate woodgrains such as bird's eye maple, only slightly different tools and techniques are used from other woodgrain methods. Most important, the base colour and glazes must be very close in tone, like caramel and honey over cream, or muted blues over pale blue-green, and the texturing must be carried out with a light and cautious hand.

Materials: Glazes or thinned oil-based paints; tinters or artists' oil paints; a small round stiff glue brush cut off squarely about ½in (12mm) above the head; a fine, pointed camel's hair brush; a clean 3in (75mm) brush to paint on the glaze; white spirit; rags or paper towels for cleaning.

Before beginning: Prepare the piece for decorating as described on pages 10 – 17, choosing a light base in the same colour family as the glazes to be used for graining. As the maple finish is very smooth, special care must be taken in preparing the surface so that it is free from scratches and small holes which would otherwise show up in the final piece. Mix colours as described on page 121.

Method: Brush a light coat of glaze over the base. When it is dry, brush on a second coat of glaze, slightly darker than the

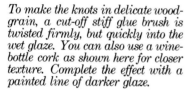

To make the knots in delicate woodgrain, a cut-off stiff glue brush is twisted firmly, but quickly into the wet glaze. You can also use a wine-bottle cork as shown here for closer texture. Complete the effect with a painted line of darker glaze.

first. Immediately, take the prepared glue brush and twist it quickly and firmly into the wet glaze to form a round knot. Continue to twist knots over the surface, spacing them out generously but irregularly, until a pleasing arrangement is made. Finish by dipping the fine camel's hair brush in the darker glaze and painting a fine half-circle around each knot. Obviously smaller or larger knots can be made by using smaller or larger brushes.

Soft honey colours will give a realistic effect, but the bird's eye texture is very striking in brilliant fantasy colours, like magenta, emerald, and bright sapphire which would all give dramatic, jewel-like finishes. Soft pinks or blues would go well in a romantic bathroom or bedroom.

Bold Woodgrain

Boldly painted woodgrains, such as this dramatic bath grained to relate to a magnificent Victorian burled wood wardrobe, needs only enthusiasm and patience to carry off well. Once again, it is a finish which looks spectacular in either natural browny wood tones or in flamboyant fantasy colours. Choose what fits the setting in which the piece will finally go.

This time the knots and whorls are hand-painted—and the looser and more vigorous the brush strokes, the more pleasing the final effect. It helps to have a real piece of the woodgrain at hand; even a good photograph will do. Most important is the knot itself, as this is the focus of the pattern. The grains are heavier and bolder near the knot, more delicate as they move further away.

When painting bold woodgrain, keep the lines loose and free-flowing, curling round the central knot in light, meandering strokes. You can even use two shades of wood tone as you become more ambitious.

Right: delicate woodgrain gives a gentle, faux bird's-eye maple effect. Below: bold woodgrain covers the panels surrounding the bath, imitating the burled grain of the Victorian wardrobe which dominates the room.

Materials: Glazes or thinned oil paints; tinters or artists' oil paints; 3in (75mm) brush for glazes; a clean 2in (50mm) brush; pointed camel's hair brushes in various sizes to suit the delicacy or boldness of the graining desired; rags or paper towelling for cleaning.

Before beginning: Prepare the piece for decorating as directed on pages 10–17. Mix colours as explained on page 121.

Method: The knot is drawn first, dipping the thicker of the camel's hair brushes in the thinned paint or glaze, and gently painting an irregular circle. The rings surrounding the knot are added next; the upper section with one brush stroke, and the lower with a second stroke. The points where these two strokes join can be whisked slightly with the dry 3in (75mm) brush to soften and mute them, if desired. Continue working, imitating the natural flow of the woodgrain. Switch to the finer artists' camel's hair brushes as you work further and further away from the knot.

Space the second knot realistically away from the first, and repeat the procedure.

The most important element in successful woodgraining is variety. The patterning must not look too regular or even, it must meander gently just as real woodgrain wanders, growing bolder and softer with a natural irregularity.

When the glaze is completely dry, protect with two or more coats of mid-sheen polyurethane, sanding down between each coat, as always.

Drawn Woodgrain

There is a third woodgraining method which is simple to master. In this technique, a coat of glaze is laid onto a pale base and then dragged with a dry brush in a gently waving pattern. The lines are then smudged lightly with a dry brush as in the combed woodgraining described (pp51—52). Using the edge of an old wine bottle cork, the lines of knot and graining are then drawn in by cutting through the glaze, following the same pattern as hand-painted woodgraining.

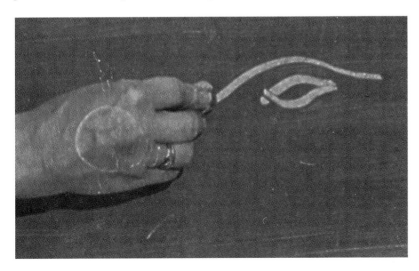

Woodgrain lines are drawn in the smudged, but still wet glaze, with an old wine-bottle cork.

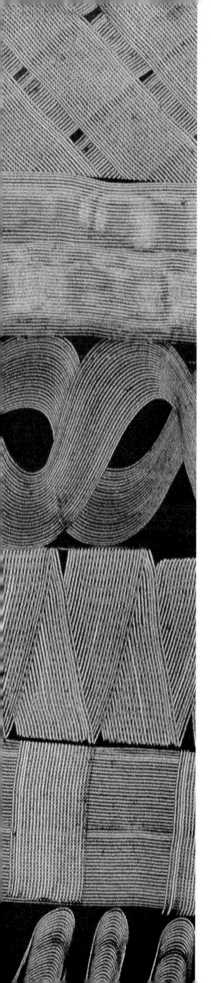

Comb Painting

Comb painting is one of the easiest and most versatile of decorative techniques. Swift, smoothly flowing strokes give the best effects, and because the glaze can be wiped off and reapplied almost endlessly, you can experiment again and again, wiping off each attempt and trying out various strokes and combinations of patterns until you feel confident.

Comb checkerboard patterns, zig-zags, graceful wiggles like those in Victorian copperplate, scallops like the edge of a lace curtain, swirls, or lay one stroke over another for intricate effects. Vary the pattern even further with different widths for the teeth of the comb, cutting them broad and widely spaced for more drama, fine and closely packed for delicacy.

Colour can be dramatic or delicate too. Muted, earthy shades are usually associated with combed furniture but many decorators today like to comb in bright candy colours. Strong, bold shades like cobalt or grass green over white can make the plainest blanket chest an eye-catching focal point.

Before beginning, think back to the scratch pictures you made as a child, by covering paper with bright crayon, coating it with black paint, then scratching through the paint to make a magical picture. Comb painting is basically the same thing. Paint on one colour and then, when it's dry, cover it with another colour. Immediately, before the second coat dries, take the comb and scratch a pattern in the wet paint.

All the patterns illustrated here (and the chest on page 44) were decorated with just one tool—the basic graining comb sold at professional paint stores. You can make your own comb, and home-made versions allow even more flexibility, as the sizes of the teeth and the width between them can be varied.

You can 'comb' with other tools as well; the American primitives used dry corn cobs, feathers, corks, fingers and anything else that caught their fancy. Do the same, using an ordinary pocket comb, a ridged pan scraper, a crinkled potato chip cutter, a square of corrugated board, or any other gadget that gives an interesting effect. All it takes is a sense of adventure and a little practice.

Almost any plain piece of furniture with a flat surface is suitable for comb painting. A chest, a wardrobe, a filing cabinet or a table are all equally good candidates, and any mouldings or carved trims can be treated with dragged and wiped decoration to give variety to the final effect.

You can use one combed design all over the piece or mix several patterns together, but a few basic principles must be kept in mind:
- Combing shows up every nick and imperfection in the surface, so care must be taken in preparing the piece for

decorating. Thorough filling and sanding is essential.

- As in other decorative techniques, most of the time will be spent in planning the decoration; that is, in deciding which pattern or combination of patterns will go where for the best overall effect. Once the decisions are made, the work should go quite quickly.
- If you wish to use straight bands of combing for edgings, do so, but don't try to edge a series of drawers, for example, with straight bands. No hand is absolutely steady and while irregular checkerboards or squiggles have naive charm, shaky stripes look amateurish.
- Remember to work in small sections. This way, you can comb the pattern to your satisfaction, wiping away any mistakes and trying again before the glaze dries. Drawers are best removed and combed one at a time, but don't forget to plan their decoration in keeping with the completed piece.

Materials: Oil-based, mid-sheen paint; an old plastic bottle with one fairly flat side or professional graining combs; scumbling glaze (see page 121); stainers (tinting colours); 3in (75mm) brush; white spirits; old rags for cleaning.

Making your own comb: Take the empty plastic container, and, using the side with the flattest area, cut a 2½in (62mm) square. On one edge of this square, using a sharp pencil, make a series of marks $\frac{1}{10}$in (2.5mm) apart. Cut 1in (25mm) deep along these marks (rule a guide-line, if necessary), then make a second series of cuts next to the first to make the teeth. This method will produce twenty-four fine teeth similar to those on the professional graining comb which was used for the effects illustrated. If you would like wider teeth, or more space between them, simply mark your square accordingly. Larger teeth and spacing will give bolder, more obvious lines.

Method: Your first comb painted piece will show more confidence and skill if a bit of time is devoted to experimenting first. Take a small piece of board on which to practice—chipboard or a smooth plank will do—and sand and paint ready for decoration (pages 10—17). Give the final coat of paint at least 24 hours to dry before combing over it.

When the board is prepared, brush on a top coat of glaze and immediately, while the glaze is still very wet, begin to run the comb along the surface, pressing it down firmly. At first, don't try to do anything special; just get the feel of it, wiping out each batch of markings with a soft cloth dampened with white spirits and brushing on a fresh coat of glaze. Try to achieve a smooth, flowing stroke and don't be afraid to move quickly. Above all, don't stop or hesitate in the middle, as the flow will be broken. Better to finish the line and if you don't like it, wipe it out and start again.

There is just one important thing to remember: keep a firm and constant pressure on the combing tool from the beginning to the end of each stroke. When you first begin to comb, the results are so quick and satisfying that you may lighten the pressure from excitement and then wonder what happened to your line.

Previous page: the number of patterns and textures which can be combed are almost endless. This sample board gives a dozen, created with a standard, professional comb. Changing the spread and width of the teeth on a home-made comb makes the possibilities literally endless. Make your own sampler before you begin to work; then you will see what can be done with the specific colours and textures you have chosen.

Comb-Painted Chest

A soft, pretty look was planned for this chest which was to be used in a room hung with bright patchwork. The colours were strong and fresh and so a clear green over white were chosen for the combing, with a combination of delicate wiggly strokes to give a gentle, lacy effect.

Red or bright blue over white would have worked equally well, especially for a child's room and a more subtle mixture of

Below left: brushing on the glaze.
Centre: straight bands of combing follow the edge of the chest.
Right: the wiggly border is made by moving the comb slightly to the right and left as the band is drawn.

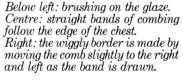

pale blue over peach or chocolate over aquamarine would take the chest into a simpler, more sophisticated setting.

Materials: As on page 52.

Method: On this chest, the combed decoration began on the side. (There was no particular reason; it could have begun on the top or the drawers equally easily.) The delicate, country Victorian mood was set by combing a lacy squiggle all around the outer edge, forming a square, frilly border with a curve and a dip at the bottom. The raised panel in the centre was given a more restrained squiggle running from the top, with straight, slightly overlapping bands of combing covering the inset panels at each side.

The drawers had a smaller version of the squiggle, a tight, carefully overlapped zig-zag that gave a slight herringbone feeling. The indented mouldings framing each drawer were simply brushed with glaze and then had their edges wiped (with a white spirit-dampened cloth wrapped tightly around one finger) to give a crisp, neat finish. The drawer frames themselves were simply brushed with glaze, and the ridged mouldings at each side of the front of the chest were brushed with glaze and then wiped to bring the ridges into relief.

As there was so much pattern on the rest of the chest, it was decided to leave the top comparatively plain. A simple, loose squiggle gave a pretty lacelike border, as if a tray cloth had been laid on top.

To finish: The glaze was left to dry completely once the combing was finished. (This can take up to a week, depending on the climate.) When it was dry, the design was covered with at least two coats of clear polyurethane varnish. The first coat was very gently rubbed down with fine sandpaper before the second coat was applied.

A matt or semi-gloss varnish generally looks better on decorated furniture than a high-gloss varnish. The recommended glaze gives a lovely, translucent effect and is easy to work with. However, if a flatter, more opaque colour is preferred, use mid-sheen oil-based paint, thinned with white spirit, if necessary, to bring it to the right combing consistency.

Below left: the comb (whether a purchased, professional tool or homemade) is always held at right angles to the surface.
Below centre: a delicate zig-zag stroke is made by moving the comb up and down slightly as it is pulled through the glaze.
Below right: the edges are wiped with a cloth dampened in white spirit and wrapped tightly around the forefinger.

Left: corner detail, showing the lace-like interplay of pattern.
Below: the completed chest of draw-ers, gentle and pretty in its fresh green and white.

Marbling

Marbling is easier to master than one would guess by looking at it. Very basically, it is a combination of colourwashing and sponging, with graining lines brushed on by hand and then softened much in the way of the accent lines in combed woodgraining. The colouring can be natural—in any of the rich, earthy tones found in real marble—or totally mad depending on the final setting of the decorated piece and the effect to be achieved. Surprisingly, marbling can be very effective when it has only the slightest resemblance to real marble.

It helps if you think of faux or fake marble in two ways. First, as the painstakingly careful rendering of authentic texturing and graining, achieved by long study and practice aimed at literally fooling the eye into taking the false for the real. The second approach is the one which we shall be concerned with here, and the one most interior decorators prefer—marbling as fantasy, a lighthearted interpretation of marble patterning and colour, which can still trick the eye into mistaking it, fleetingly, for the real thing.

Faux marble is perhaps most effective where real marble might have been used, such as the top of a chest or table, or surrounding a fireplace. But it is much more interesting in an unexpected context—covering basic kitchen cupboards, transforming a second-hand filing cabinet, or turning a great, ugly lump of a chest into an amazing objet d'art sectioned in faux marble of many colours.

Below left: a sheet of loosely crumpled newspaper is dropped onto the wet glaze.
Below right: when the paper is lifted away, a creased, marble-like texture results. The crumpled newspaper is turned to reveal a clean section and then dropped onto the wet glaze again until the desired amount of marbling is achieved.

The quickest way of recreating the random, cracking lines of marble is to brush on a coat of glaze, and then drop a loosely crumpled rag or piece of newspaper onto the wet colour, lifting it away, turning it to reveal a clean section and dropping it again until the folds of rag or paper have made a loose, wrinkled pattern in the glaze.

A similar method is to put a creased and then re-opened piece of newspaper on top of the glaze, and then pounce this newspaper at random with a small, stiff brush. When the newspaper is lifted away, the surface will be dappled where the brush was used, with slight vein-like lines left by the paper creases. As the paint dries, extra veins can be squiggled in with a fine brush and paler areas pulled out with a clean sponge and white spirit.

Simple marbling can be achieved by painting in the veins lightly onto the plain ground colour, then blurring them slightly with a dry brush (as with the combed woodgraining on page 52), or with a piece of sponge soaked in white spirit, then adding a second set of veining in a second colour. Caramel and grey veining is effective over white or cream, or try soft green and red umber over pale honey. As each set of veining is blurred and softened, the brush and sponge can be used to dab extra little bits of colour in the plain sections, to imitate the irregularity of real marble.

It is not even necessary to imitate natural veining precisely to achieve a pretty, marble-like look. One London interior decorator laid down a pale coat of cream, sponged on a delicately variegated honey-toned surface in the same technique as for the marbled washstand described (page 59) —and then added delicate little squiggles of colour like tiny glow-worms wiggling erratically over the surface. The colours are always pale—soft blue, pink, yellow, mauve—using either thinned gouache or acrylic paints for the clearest, freshest colouring, and painted on with a fine camel's hair brush.

Yet another simple means of achieving a pretty, marbled look is to lay on irregular patches of glaze over a pale ground, filling in the open areas with a second, slightly different shade. Tobacco and grey over white would be one good choice, or sea blue and emerald over cream. Immediately go over the entire surface with a clean natural sponge or crumpled paper towelling to soak up some of the glaze and soften the colour. Then take up some white spirit on a clean brush and spatter the glaze generously. Little holes will open up wherever the white spirit falls. Follow this, if you like, with a light spattering of methylated spirit which will give a slightly different effect, and blur again with the sponge or paper towelling.

As with woodgraining, it helps to have pictures or pieces of real marble nearby as reference, but it is important not to be constrained by it. As long as the result is pleasing, faux marble doesn't have to look exactly like the real thing.

When the paint is completely dry—taking up to a week in wet weather—protect with two or more coats of polyurethane varnish, sanding between each coat.

Far left: imaginative marbling in many colours makes a showstopping centrepiece out of an old eyesore.

Near left: simple marbling turns an old filing cabinet into a sophisticated accent for any room.

Below left: soft marbling covers cheap built-in kitchen units; an unexpected and sensational effect.

Left and below: a plain pine washstand gets a trompe l'oeil marble top in rich terra cotta and cream. Soft greys with sand would have been a good alternative.

Marbled Washstand

Below top left: sketchy lines are criss-crossed lightly over the plain paint.
Top right: when the lines are dry, a pale glaze is brushed on.
Lower left: the same brush is used to roughen the surface lightly.
Lower right: a bit of natural sponge lifts off irregularly shaped patches of glaze.

Materials: Thinned oil-based paint or glaze; artists' oil colours or tinters; a brush for laying on the coloured glaze; a natural marine sponge; a fine artist's camel's hair brush; newspaper; clean rags; white spirit; jam jars (one for each colour); saucer.

Before beginning: Prepare the piece for decorating as described on pages 10—17. The base colour is most often pale—white, cream, pale grey, beige—but can be any colour, depending on the desired effect. In early experiments, however, it would be easier to work with a pale base. The washstand illustrated was painted cream.

Method: First, a small blob of oil paint is squeezed into the saucer and thinned with white spirit to the consistency of

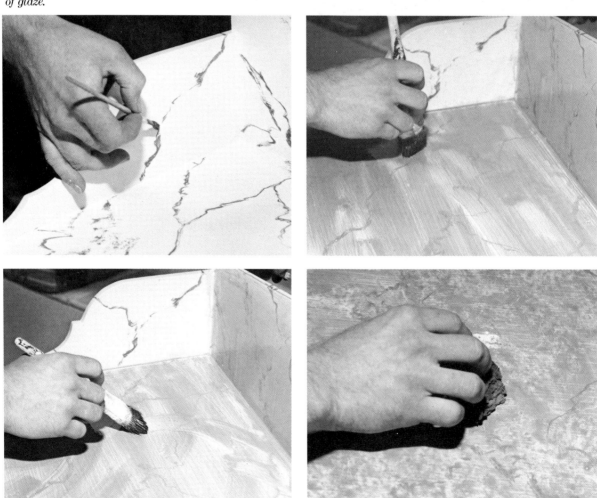

cream. Using the fine artist's brush, sketchy, meandering, wobbly lines are criss-crossed delicately over the surface, imitating the natural lining look of real marble, and then softened immediately by dabbing at them lightly with a tiny piece of natural sponge. When these lines are dry, a soft coloured glaze is brushed on lightly. The same brush is then swept randomly over the surface to roughen it slightly. A small piece of sponge is dabbed and rolled over the surface, lifting off irregularly shaped bits of glaze. The same bit of sponge is then dipped into the saucer of thinned oil paint, squeezed out tightly, and after having been tested on a bit of waste paper to make sure the paint is sparse enough, dabbed lightly here and there on the sponged surface to add occasional highlights. A second, absolutely clean bit of sponge is squeezed out tightly in clean white spirit and also dabbed here and there on the sponged surface to pull up the creamy highlights. When this has dried slightly, the artist's brush is dipped again into the thinned oil paint, and the bristles squeezed out between the fingers and spread out into a spatula shape. The flat of the bristles are then brushed lightly along the graining lines made earlier, to give a delicate, hazy but strongly coloured accent.

Below, top left: the same bit of sponge is dipped into the thinned paint, squeezed out and dabbed onto the surface to add highlights.
Top right: accent lines are added over the graining lines made earlier, with the brush pressed firmly into a spatula shape.
Lower left: the sponge is used to remove excess paint from the artist's brush.
Lower right: brushing lightly across the graining lines to give a hazy accent.

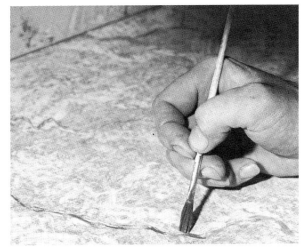

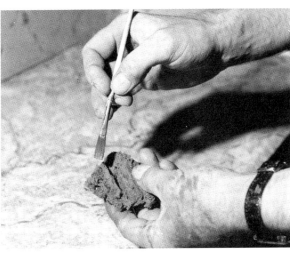

Far right: an old wooden office desk gaily stencilled with flowers and geometrics.
Right: urns filled with flowering vines cover the stained wood doors of this chest.
Below right: simple dining-room table stencilled to match the flower chintz covering the walls (see instructions on following pages).
Below left: kitchen cabinets happily stencilled with butter-flies and flowers.

STENCILLING

Stencilling is as easy as any of the other decorative techniques in this book, but it needs more in the way of planning and preparation before you begin. It's just like making a dress; you choose the colour and fabric, pattern and style, then cut out all the pieces, pin them together and fit the dress before beginning to sew. Stencilling is the same. Choose the design and tranfser it to card, then cut it out and plan exactly how it will work on the piece of furniture, before picking up the stencil brush.

After that, however, it's easy. Stencilling is very similar to pouncing on. Dip a small, stiff brush into a bit of paint and tap it onto the surface through the cut-out stencil. When the pattern is lifted away, the stencilled design remains.

Almost any simple piece of furniture can be stencilled: an old wooden office desk, the baby's cot, a dining-room table, even ordinary kitchen or bathroom cabinets. And anything can become a stencil design, from the richly flowered chintz on the dining-room walls to a much-loved picture from a child's favourite story book. All it takes is imagination, and the friendly local photocoyping machine.

Photocopiers can be magical tools. The best will blow up or reduce an image as they copy it and then print it onto almost any kind of paper or card. Used cleverly, they're ideal stencilling tools and are as handy as the local quick copy shop. Have your fabric or picture blown up or reduced to the size required and printed onto stiff stencil card. Then all you need to do is cut it out.

The best thing about stencilling is that it's such enormous fun, letting you create—without any great talent or sums of cash—a colourful and totally personal look made up of all your favourite things. If you love flowers, cover the kitchen cabinets with them, taking the stencils from fabrics or from references at the local library or museum. Throw a Navajo rug over an old table, stencilling the design from a picture in a magazine or the catalogue from an exhibition. Give your child a Dr Doolittle chest, lifting the stencil from his picture book—or stencil her play-table with the letters of the alphabet and an animal to go with each, taking the figures from a Victorian alphabet book or an old frieze. Simplest of all, take an odd collection of wooden chairs, paint them all the same colour and stencil your initials on the back (taking the letters from an old embroidery book), creating a matched set to go round your dining-room table.

The risk is that once you've made your stencil, you may want to use it everywhere! Like a child with a new toy, you'll be tempted to tuck a little stencilled flower here, and a row of ducks there. Restrain yourself, as careful planning is the most important part of stencilling successfully. But apart from that, have a wonderful time.

Making the Stencil

Materials: Stencil card (available at good art supply shops); stencil knife or Stanley knife with a fine blade.

First, choose your design. Almost any picture or geometric pattern can be made to work effectively in stencil form, as long as the pattern is reduced to its simplest forms. The table used as an example (page 76) was stencilled with daisies and lilies from the flowered chintz covering the dining-room walls.

The chintz has soft bouquets of flowers and buds running through the design, and this was chosen for a border around the top of the table. A length of fabric with this floral design was taken to the local photocopy shop and reproduced on the largest machine in order to print the complete repeat. This first test pattern was taken back and laid onto the table to check the size and to confirm that the design would in fact work as planned.

Note: an ordinary office photocopier usually will only copy onto its own paper, but almost any copying service can reproduce your pattern onto paper, card, or even transparent acetate which can be used for see-through stencils, although they must be cut with a designer's scalpel and handled very carefully.

If it had been decided to enlarge the flowers, the first test print would have been blown-up on the enlarging copier. In the same way, if the flowers looked better in a smaller size, the same machine would have reduced the print.

Once the print is the right size, simply photocopy it onto the heavy stencil card. Keep this test print in case it is needed to run off more copies on the stencil card.

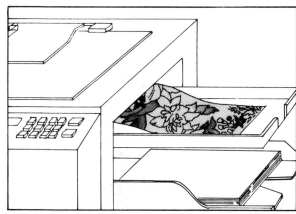

Above left: the flowered chintz from which the design is taken.
Above right: reproducing the print onto stencil card, using the photocopier.

Planning the Design

This is the trickiest part of the entire process, because it is here that you will decide which parts of the pattern to keep and which to ignore. Several stencils can be used on top of each other to make complicated patterns, but each individual stencil will have its own part of the design cut simply.

Only the most basic elements of this rather intricate floral pattern were used for the stencil—the petals of the lilies, the pointed leaves surrounding the central cluster and the heart of the chrysanthemum in the middle. The sprays of leaves connecting each little bouquet of flowers were also reduced to basics—thin stems, clustered buds, star-like flowerets. As each shape was decided, it was outlined with a felt-tip pen so that the final design could be seen clearly, and any adjustments made.

Cutting the Stencil

The printed stencil card is laid onto an ordinary cutting board and the shapes cut with a stencil knife or the fine blade of a Stanley knife. Begin to cut anywhere on the design, holding the knife exactly as you would hold a pencil. Your other hand should rest firmly on the stencil all of the time, turning it slowly so that you are always cutting towards you. To make sure the line is smooth and steady, lift the cutting blade from the stencil as little as possible.

The blade must stay on the line of the design, not outside, nor inside it. It is also important to leave a 1 in (25mm) margin around the edge of the design to prevent the brush from smudging over the edge. When all of the shapes have been cut out, hold the stencil up to the light and look at it carefully. Make sure there are no jagged lines and no cutting inside or outside of the lines (a little variation doesn't matter unless you are planning a very complicated overlay of stencils). Make sure also that you have not left too narrow a bridge between the cut-out shapes. Too small a bridge will break as you use the stencil. When you have made any necessary corrections in the cutting, it is time to make a test proof of your design.

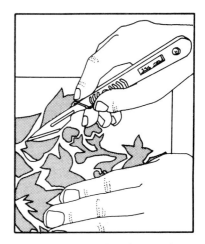

Cutting the stencil using continuous, flowing strokes of the knife.

Making the Test Proof

Materials: A sheet of plain, waste paper; stencil brush; mid-sheen oil-based paint; masking tape; china dish or saucer for the paint; clean rags or paper towelling for cleaning up; white spirit.

Method: Lay the cut stencil onto the sheet of plain paper on an absolutely flat surface. Tape the corners with masking tape to hold the stencil firmly in place.

Put a very small amount of paint in the saucer—a tablespoonful will do—and dip the stencil brush into it lightly. Tap the brush onto plain paper to make sure it is not overloaded with paint and then begin to stencil your design.

Holding the stencil flat with one hand, and with the brush held vertically in the other, tap the paint onto the paper through the cut-out shapes of the design. The technique is very similar to that of pouncing on in that the brush almost bounces up and down, but there is one important difference. In stencilling, the brush should merely tap the surface and deposit the paint as it touches. Don't press the brush down hard onto the surface so that the bristles spread, because this can

Below left: stencilling the test proof.
Right: the test proof showing the complete design before colour separation.
If you are intending to stencil a large project, and you are using two colours, it is wise to try out both colours on the proof to see how they look together.

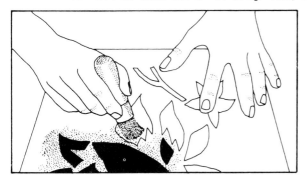

65

Above: in single stencil colour separation, the first colour is filled in (top) and then, with the same stencil in place, the second colour is added. Be careful to fill in the right place each time. Watch the colour around the edges of each space.

Below: here one stencil was used for the leaves and a second stencil for the fruit and blossom, and the third picture is a combination of the two stencils as the design will look when it is finished.

push the paint under the edges of the stencil, which spoils the cleanly cut lines.

When all of the shapes have been coloured, lift the stencil away and look at your design.

Separating the Colours

You may be happy to stencil the pattern in just one colour. But if you would prefer two or more colours in the design, you can proceed in one of two ways.

The Single Stencil Method

If the design is simple and widely spaced—a small bouquet of flowers to be stencilled onto the panels of a cupboard, a row of geese bordering a child's wardrobe—use the same stencil for all of the colours. For this, it is important to have a separate stencilling brush for each colour and it helps to have the smallest brushes available. A dish or saucer for each colour is also needed.

Tape the stencil firmly onto a clean sheet of scrap paper. Beginning with the main colour, dip the brush into the paint and, after testing the brush on a piece of waste paper, stencil in all of the areas in which this colour is to be used. Take care that the brush doesn't stray into areas intended for another colour.

When the colouring is completed, allow the paint to dry for a moment or two and then take the second brush and fill in the second most important colour. Continue with each additional colour until the design is complete. Then lift the stencil away so that you can see the finished effect.

This single stencil method can also be used for more subtle colouring, when one or more tones shade and overlap for a softer, gentler look. In this case, colours are deliberately stencilled over each other to mute the edges and give the design greater variety and texture.

The Multiple Stencil Method

If the design is very detailed or if the cut-out shapes are close to one another, the pattern will work better if you make a colour separation, that is, individual stencils for each colour to be

used. It is not at all difficult, but once again it takes time and careful planning.

Start by making a test pattern using the original cut-out design. Following the single stencil method, try out the colours until you are happy with the finished design. Don't worry at this point about any overlapping of colour. This will be corrected with your colour separation.

Cut a piece of stencil card in the same size as the original, making one for each colour in the design. Tape the original cut-out stencil over one of the newly trimmed pieces and, using a sharp pencil, trace each shape in the main colour, then remove. Repeat for the second and any additional colours.

Above: in a continuous border, one element of the design can be used as a register mark in placing the stencil.

Eliminating Bridges in the Design

One advantage of multiple stencils is that you can use them to eliminate the bridges between elements of the design. In the flower border, for example, the daisy buds nestle right up against their stalks. Wonderfully sophisticated effects can be stencilled in this way, with subtly shaded flowers drooping realistically over their leaves or planes apparently flying in and out of clouds.

Have the photocopier print one copy of your design onto plain paper and then one copy on stencil card for each colour you intend to use.

The first, plain paper copy will be your key. Colour it in with felt-tip pens or paints in the combination that pleases you most. With this as your guide, cut out each stencil, making one for each of the colours in the design. Be careful to follow the printed lines very carefully, cutting on the line precisely and not inside nor outside of it. Careful cutting ensures that your colours will be printed exactly as you want them to be.

When each stencil is cut and marked with register marks and numbers, make your test proof. Any changes or corrections must be done at this stage.

Register Marks

To make sure each stencil is placed correctly for printing, you will need to add register marks. There are two ways of doing this. The simplest method is to repeat one element on each side of the design on every stencil. For example, as shown above right, a daisy at each end of the design was cut on every stencil. When the second and third stencils were placed for printing, it was easy to see the correct position very quickly. The same daisies were used to position the first or key stencil to repeat the design in a continuous border. The only drawback in this method is that you must not print the register shape (the daisy) in the wrong colour.

When using complex shapes, make the key stencil first for the major colour. On all other stencils add broken cuts as windows around the edges of the first shapes; when these are placed over the design you will see the edges clearly.

The last step is to mark the top of each stencil and number each in the order they are to be printed.

A multiple stencil, of a second or third colour, showing the broken lines of register 'windows'. The gaps in the lines should remind you not to colour them in. With acetate stencils you may not need such precise registers unless they become opaque with surplus paint; see next page.

Clear Acetate Stencils

If the design is needed for a lot of stencilling, such as taking the flower border around the walls, acetate stencils will last much longer than those made out of heavy card, and are also much easier to keep clean. Rolls of acetate or other stiff transparent sheeting are available cut to size from most good art supply shops or graphic arts suppliers, and you can choose whatever size you need.

Materials: Transparent acetate sheeting cut to the same size as the design, in anything from .005 to .010 gauge, depending on the stiffness and durability desired. (Ask the advice of your graphic arts supplier.) If the design has more than one colour, you will need one sheet cut to size for each colour in the design. Also, a fine point permanent felt-tip pen, masking tape and stencil knife.

Method: As before, have the photocopier print the design in the correct size on plain paper. Colour it in with felt-tip pens or paints until you are happy with the way it looks. Then lay the coloured design on a flat, well-lit surface—a large cutting board on a table will do—and tape it down firmly. Lay the clear plastic sheet on top and tape it down tightly as well. If you have bought the acetate in a roll, lay it so that it curves down.

If the design is in one colour only, trace all of the design with the permanent felt-tip pen, making sure to leave bridges between each element in the motif. Leave a 1 in (25mm) border as well, to make sure the brush doesn't smudge around the edges.

If there is more than one colour, trace the most important shade on this first, or key, sheet. As always in multiple stencil designs, follow the lines precisely, making bridges only between elements placed next to each other on the same stencil.

When the first colour is completely traced, lay the second sheet of acetate carefully on top, matching all the sides, and tape it down firmly. Using the felt-tip permanent pen, trace the second colour. Repeat this process with any additional colours.

Register marks are easy to make on clear acetate stencils. The simplest way is to make a small cross at each corner. As the second and subsequent stencils are traced, these crosses are traced as well.

Cutting the Stencil

Remove all of the traced stencils from the cutting board, along with the paper original. Lay the first stencil onto the cutting board and cut in the same way as for a heavy card stencil, following the lines precisely and remembering always to cut towards you, lifting the blade as little as possible to maintain a smooth, even line. Repeat with any additional stencils in the design. When all of the stencils are cut, print a test proof on waste paper.

Paints for Stencilling

There is no need to use special paints for stencilling furniture.

Ordinary oil-based, mid-sheen paint works perfectly well. And since you need very little paint for stencilling—the tiniest bit covers a great deal of territory—buy a small tin of white as the base and use artists' oil paints or tinters to colour a half teacup of whatever colours you need. The floral bordered table was stencilled in just this way.

Materials: White oil-based, mid-sheen paint; tinters or artists' oil paints for each colour; small glass jam jars with lids, one for each colour; small sticks or plastic spoons for stirring; white spirit; clean rags or paper towelling for cleaning up.

Method: Put five or six tablespoonfuls of white paint into one of the jam jars and add tinter a little at a time, stirring thoroughly after each addition and testing the colour on a bit of scrap paper. Repeat for each additional colour. If you are making deep shades, you may find that the paint gets very thick indeed, almost like porridge, but don't worry. Paint for stencilling should be thick—ideally the consistency is rather like heavy cream—but even if the brush can stand up in the paint, it will be fine for stencilling. When all of the colours are mixed, do a careful test proof to make sure they all work. When you have finished, screw the jar tops on tightly to keep the paints moist.

Planning the Design

Once you are satisfied with your stencil design and have mixed all of the colours and tested them, it is time to plan exactly how the design will be placed on the piece of furniture. By this stage you should have a clear idea of the overall look you are trying to achieve, but now the exact position of the design, joining of corners or the repeat of borders must be meticulously worked out in every detail.

It's possible to go ahead and put the design wherever you'd like to see it, without careful planning, and this kind of artless, casual positioning can be charmingly naive. If this is the effect you want, stencil your motifs or borders directly onto the painted or smoothly sanded wood surface and skip the planning stage completely.

Placing by Proof
Most of the time, it helps to test out the total design. If you are using individual motifs scattered all over the surface of a table or chest of drawers, stencil several paper proofs and move them around on the surface until you are happy with the arrangement. Secure each paper proof with a bit of masking tape and when you begin to work, simply replace each proof with the stencil.
Tape test proofs in place to see whether your design works as you have planned. In placing individual motifs, simply remove the test proof and replace it with the cut stencil when you are ready to begin stencilling your design.

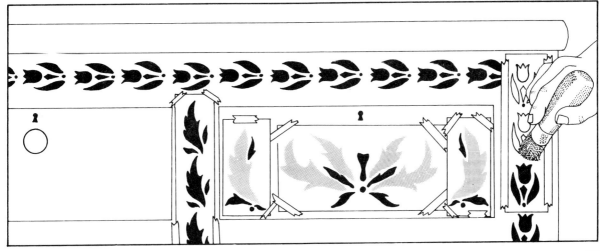

Borders

If you are stencilling a continuously running border, such as the floral border, you will have to figure out how many times the repeat will fit into the area. Measure the width of a single repeat of the design and then measure the length of the area it is to run along. Divide the width of the design by the length of the area; this will give you the number of repeats. Be sure to include any spaces between motifs, if there are to be any.

Mark a chalk or light pencil guideline along the length of the surface, to keep the line of the border straight, and make corresponding placement (positioning) marks on the stencil. After calculating the number of repeats, make marks along the surface guideline to show where each repeat should be placed. Make these marks on your proof, before stencilling the proof, and any corrections in the spacing on the proof must be repeated on the actual surface to be decorated.

For a border, you will need to stencil a complete paper proof in the same size as the surface to be decorated. On this proof, you will turn corners, plan the exact placement of each motif, solve any unexpected problems, and generally make sure that the entire design works as you have planned. This may seem like a lot of work, but it is worth the effort, as by the time you actually begin to stencil you can be sure that the design is absolutely right.

Borders can be easily cornered by mitring the design (far left) or butting the two bands of pattern together (near left). Some overlapping of motif doesn't matter and often enhances the design.

Turning Corners

Borders that lead into corners can be handled in several ways:

- Butt the design at the corner, placing it at right angles to the adjoining corner.
- Mitre the corner of the design by drawing a diagonal line from the inner to the outer corner of the border and placing masking tape tightly along one side of this line. Stencil up to the tape, then remove the tape and place it on the other side of the diagonal line. Now stencil up to the tape from the other direction.
- Piece the corner by filling in shapes from various parts of the design to carry the pattern around the corner without interruption. This solution works particularly well with borders using a vine motif.
- Use a special corner piece, possibly an element from the border or from another part of the overall design. In this case it is important to stencil the corner pieces first, and then stencil the border design to meet them.

Placement Marks

When making a continuous border, such as a floral border, placement marks have to be made at each end of the repeat. These are the same as register marks, but are put onto the first stencil only. They are placed at each end of the design so that

Curving vines can simply wind around the the corner (near right), while special corner motifs inserted at the end of each border strip (far right) can be the focus of attention rather than the border itself.

Right: mark pencil guidelines to keep the line straight and position each motif.

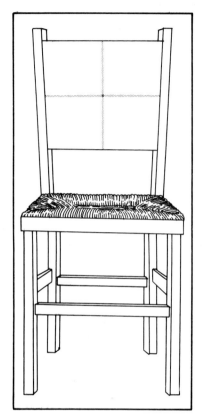

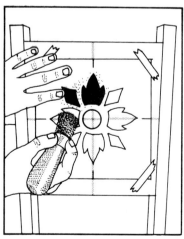

Placement on a chairback. Mark the centre of the surface in pencil (top), then place your stencil motif in place over the crossed lines.

you can move in either direction when printing.

To make the marks on a card stencil, take your test proof and lay it on the cutting board. Using the stencil knife, cut placement marks carefully on each side of the design. Take the first stencil and lay it on the cutting board next to the test proof as if you were ready to make the next print. Let the test proof overlap the stencil, tape it firmly and trace the cut-out placement mark. Remove the test proof and cut the placement mark into the stencil. Repeat for the placement mark on the other side.

If you are using a clear plastic stencil, take your test proof and move the clear stencil over it as if you were about to make the next print. Trace the placement shapes onto the clear plastic with the permanent felt-tip pen and, removing the test pattern, cut them out carefully with the stencil knife.

Guidelines

If you want to place a stencil in the exact centre of a chest or table, or space an allover design precisely, you will need to draw guidelines. These lines can be sketched lightly on the surface to be decorated in pencil or chalk so that they can be removed easily, and onto the stencil in pen.

Centring the Design

To centre a design, first make two pencil lines dividing the surface to be decorated in half horizontally and vertically: the lines will cross in the centre. Make the same marks on the stencil with a cross in the centre of the design and bring the lines out to the edge. With a clear plastic stencil, these lines will be placed exactly over those on the surface as you print. With a card stencil, position the design by matching the vertical and horizontal lines at the edge of the stencil with those on the surface to be decorated.

Placing an Allover Design

To position an allover design correctly, a grid will have to be drawn on the surface to be stencilled. Start by establishing the centre (as above). Then centre each of the four sections in the same way and then each of the subsequent 16 sections. Continue to centre each section until each crossed line is as far from the next cross as each motif will be placed. (If the grid has been carefully measured, the crosses will be equidistant from each other.) For example: if you want just a few fairly large motifs well spaced out, you may need to mark only an eight square grid. If, however, you have a small motif which is to be repeated frequently, the grid may need to include 16 or even 32 squares in order to establish the correct spacing.

This method produces a squared grid on a square or round table, but on a rectangular surface, the grid will repeat the shape of the rectangle. To produce a squared grid on a rectangular surface, the method is slightly different. Centre the surface as before. Then, moving horizontally across the top, divide each panel in half vertically. Repeat, until the lines are spaced apart as far as you wish. Now measure the distance between each vertical line. Then, starting with the centre line made at the beginning, mark and draw horizontal lines across the surface the same distance apart as the vertical lines. This will give a correctly squared grid.

Stencilling in Difficult Areas

Sometimes stencils cannot be placed flat because a moulding or some other obstacle is in the way. If the stencil isn't completely flat, the print will be fuzzy or incomplete. There are two ways to solve this problem.

Bend the stencil: Paper or very thin plastic stencils can be folded at the edge of the design so that the margin can be placed tightly against the obstacle while the design lies flat on the surface. Heavier plastic cannot bend smoothly, so you will have to hinge it. Put a ruler against the stencil about ⅛in (3mm) from the edges of the design. Cut along the edge of the ruler with the stencil knife or Stanley knife. Keeping the two pieces fitted together, place transparent tape over the entire length of the cut on both sides of the stencil. The strip is now hinged and can be bent easily.

Cut a small stencil: Duplicate whatever parts of the design cannot be placed flat on a separate, small stencil. Fit these little stencils close to the moulding or overhang and cover any parts of the surface that might be smudged with masking tape.

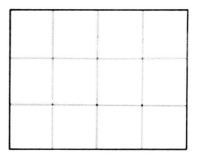

Grid for an allover design.

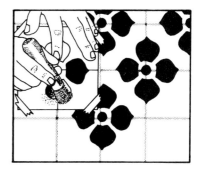

Placing the motif.

The completed design.

Left: bent stencil and small stencil.

73

If neither bending nor cutting a stencil (as described on page 73) works satisfactorily in a particular situation, you can always fill in the design by hand, using a fine camel's hair brush and thinning the paint slightly with white spirit so that it flows more smoothly.

Blocking Out and Filling In

Sometimes you may want to omit part of the design to give a bit of variation to the pattern. Simply cover the space you do not want to print with masking tape or a piece of cardboard attached either to the stencil itself, or to the surface being printed. Remove the tape or cardboard carefully from the stencil or surface after printing.

To fill in areas at the edge of a continuous border or allover design, print small elements of the design from the stencil, blocking out unwanted areas with masking tape or cardboard. It may be better to make small, individual stencils if the space is awkward to reach.

When the proof is completed to your satisfaction, with all mistakes or flaws corrected, and any necessary guidelines drawn, begin to stencil the design.

The Stencilling Method

The actual process of stencilling is very simple. The short, fat, stiff-bristled stencil brush is dipped into a tiny amount of paint, tested on scrap paper to make sure it isn't too wet, and then tapped lightly but firmly onto the surface through the stencil so that the bristles leave a light deposit of paint.

Materials: The prepared stencils; a stencil brush for each colour of paint; the prepared jars of paint; a small dish for each colour; masking tape; scrap paper; white spirit; clean rags or paper towels for cleaning up.

Stencilling is a neat, orderly process and needs very little room to carry out. The main things to consider are good light and your own comfort, as you will be sitting or kneeling in almost the same position for quite a long time.

Before beginning: Prepare the piece for decorating as described on pages 10 — 17.

If you haven't done stencilling before, you might want to spend a little time perfecting your technique on waste paper before transferring your design to the piece of furniture. These are the points to keep in mind.

The brush is held exactly like a pencil, with the fingers close to the bristles. It is dipped lightly into the paint and then tapped onto the surface like a tiny hammer, with the wrist making the tapping movement. The arm should not rest on the surface; it swings easily from the shoulder as the brush moves over the surface. The other hand is used to hold the stencil flat so that paint doesn't creep under the edge, the fingers following the brush as it moves. Be sure to keep the tapping light; the brush should merely touch the surface and deposit the paint, not spread it around.

There should always be some variation in the shading of

the colours as they are printed, but there must be consistency as well. Be careful not to concentrate on one area at a time. Instead, work in broad, circular movements until the shapes are gradually filled in. Build up the colour very slowly; don't try to put it on thickly and then spread it around. The stencil shapes should have a sharp, crisp outline. Think in terms of outlining the shapes first and then working in towards the centre of them.

Always complete all of the stencilling in one colour before going on to the next. The work goes much faster than if you switch from one colour to another all of the time.

Correcting Mistakes

Too much paint on the stencil brush or a paint mixture that is too thin causes the paint to seep or run under the stencil. Shapes then become blurred instead of sharply defined. Always check your brush before beginning to stencil to make sure it isn't overloaded. If you do find that paint has seeped under the edge, however, don't despair. As soon as you take away the stencil and see the damage, wrap a bit of clean rag tightly around your finger and dip it into white spirit. Following the outline carefully, wipe away the smudge. If there is too much smudging to wipe away cleanly, wipe the entire section clean with white spirit and stencil that bit again.

Prints which are too pale and scantily coloured mean that your brush has had too little paint. Dip your brush into the paint again, test it carefully on waste paper and re-stencil the pale areas.

Prints that are too dark can be lightened by touching them gently with a pad of clean rag before they dry. If the paint has run under the stencil and dried before discovering it, you can scrape it away carefully with the stencil knife.

Alternatively, paint over smudges and over-runs with the base colour, using a fine camel's hair brush and thinning the paint slightly with white spirit so that it flows.

You can also replace the stencil, shifting it over slightly and stencilling that section again to cover the smudging.

Trial proofs should eliminate design errors before they reach this stage, but if a major mistake is found before the paint has dried, simply wipe the offending area away and stencil it again, correcting the error. If the paint has dried, you can always fill in unexpected gaps with small elements of the design. As with any hand craft, some inconsistencies and irregularities add to the charm.

Cleaning Up

Always clean your materials as soon as you have finished a stencilling session. Heavy card stencils cannot be cleaned as completely as plastic stencils, but wipe them down to remove surplus paint and remove the masking tape carefully. Always clean brushes immediately with white spirit and mild detergent and water. Rinse them thoroughly and put them in a small jar to dry, with the bristles pointing up.

Flowered Dining Room Table

This was a plain, modern pine table, boring but well made, which had originally been bought for the kitchen in a previous house. The new dining room had its walls covered with a pale yellow flowered cotton chintz and it was decided to paint and stencil the table to match.

The table was prepared for decorating as described on pages 10—17 and painted with three coats of pale yellow matched to the ground colour of the chintz. The stencils were prepared as described on page 64 and the colours mixed to match the colours in the fabric design.

A complete test proof was printed and during its preparation, several problems arose: for instance, the border repeat was a cluster of lilies and chrysanthemums with a spray of daisies at one side. In order to place a bouquet in each corner of the table and again at the centre of each side, parts of the design were blocked out in certain repeated prints. Also, to make the design balance at each end of the table, one cluster of blossoms was reversed or flipped over at each end.

In addition, it was decided to strengthen the design with a frame of two lines or stripes, one wider than the other, and repeat this striping with single lines on the frame and legs. Guidelines were drawn using the tip of a leaf at each end of the repeat as measuring points, and additional guidelines were drawn to centre the clusters of flowers in the corners and on each side.

Stencilling the table: The main, or key stencil in this design contained the flowers, and printing began with this. The second most important stencil contained the leaves, with the third stencil holding the accent blossom. Each stencil was taped down firmly to keep it in position, with the free hand following the brush to make sure the stencil stayed smooth. Each colour was allowed to dry to the touch before the next was stencilled.

When the floral border was complete, the framing lines were added. Masking tape, 1in (25.5mm) wide, was pressed tightly at each side of the area to be striped, following carefully measured pencil marks. When the outer line was completely taped on all sides, the colour was stencilled in. After the paint had dried to the touch, the masking tape was removed, and the lines left to dry thoroughly for the next twenty-four hours. On the following day the second, inner line was measured and taped and the second line of colour stencilled in. Because the second line of taping necessarily overlapped the first stencilled line, the paint had to dry completely before starting the second line, in case the tape lifted away the first stripe of paint when it was removed.

The same method was followed for the stripes on both the frame and legs.

Finally, it was decided to centre each panel of the frame with a small motif taken from the main design. A leaf surrounding the bouquet was chosen and traced onto stencil card. After a trial proof, the single leaf was reversed and paired with the original to make a small motif repeated on the centre of each side of the frame.

When the stencilling had dried completely, the table was protected with three coats of clear polyurethane varnish on the body, sanded lightly between each coat, with five coats covering the top. A piece of bevelled glass was cut to fit and further protect the top.

Top left: starting to stencil the main colour, the pink flowers. Top centre: stencilling the pink repeat. Top right: turning the corner. Middle left: stencilling the second colour, the green leaves. Middle centre: placing the stencil in repeat. Middle right: stencilling the third colour, the blue accent. Bottom left: all three colours complete in position. Bottom centre: stencilling the masked off border. Bottom right: filling in the side motif.

Spray Stencilling

Spray paint is used increasingly by professional and amateur stencillers both for speed and to achieve a variety of soft and textured effects. Most good art supply shops or graphics arts suppliers have a good range of spray paints and while they are more expensive to buy than ordinary paints and tinters, one tin will cover a lot of territory. While you cannot match colours precisely, the better brands usually have a wide range of shades and you can usually find one to suit your purpose.

There are three things to beware of when you are using spray paints:

- They make a mess, with spray drifting over a fairly wide area; use lots of newspaper held in place with masking tape to cover all the areas you don't want painted.
- Edges are often hazy, particularly if you haven't been careful to keep the stencil absolutely flat.

To make the Noah's Ark animals (below) spray stencil in the first colour (above).

- The paint drips and spatters because it is thin: spray as quickly as possible, in a series of short, swift puffs and stop before the surface is completely saturated. If drips do occur, wipe them away immediately or wipe the entire pattern clean and spray that section again.

Sprays allow you to do lots of things you cannot do with ordinary brush stencilling. You can make lovely, hazy designs with clouds of colour overlapping softly. You can spray light puffs of colour one over the other to create lovely, speckled textures in your design. Or you can spray gold or silver and then overspray with ordinary colour, letting the metallic sparkle come gently through the covering colour.

The easiest way to spray stencil is to place a cut-out shape on the plainly painted surface and spray over it. When the design is removed, the silhouette is revealed. Use leaves, ferns, paper doilies, coins of different shapes and sizes, or cut-out paper patterns of any kind, held firmly in place with double-sided sticky tape, and combine them to make quite complicated allover designs. Simple abstracts made of randomly cut rectangles and circles can be surprisingly effective, especially if two or three closely related colours are sprayed in a hazily marbled effect.

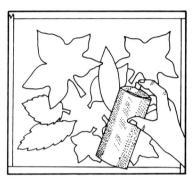

Using double-sided tape, attach the leaves onto the surface and spray in short, puffy bursts. Don't let the tape show or it will leave marks.

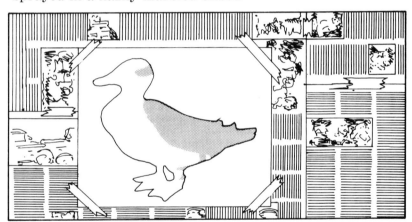

When the first colour is dry, shift the stencil and spray the second colour (above).

When the leaves are removed, a pretty pattern remains.

Both brushed and spray stencilled techniques can be combined. Spray a soft haze of colour through one stencil and then brush stencil a sharper pattern on top, or brush stencil an allover pattern and spray stencil a cloudy design over it, like a misty curtain partially obscuring the pattern beneath.

One of the prettiest effects is to hold the stencil slightly above the surface to be decorated and spray very slightly and briefly, followed by a second spray of colour using the same stencil cut in reverse. One marvellous chest was covered in this way with positive/negative leaves peeping out of a soft cloud of yellow and green.

Materials: Cans of spray paint in desired colours; stencils with extra wide borders (can be strips of paper attached to an ordinary stencil with masking tape); lots of newspaper; masking tape; white spirit; clean rags or paper towelling for cleaning up; rubber kitchen gloves to protect your hands from the spray.

Method: Holding the can 10—12in (250—300mm) away from the surface, spray in short bursts, using just enough paint to cover lightly. If the stencil is taped tightly to the surface, the outline should be clear and clean. If a hazy outline is desired, hold the stencil slightly away from the surface as you spray. Experiment on waste paper until you find the combination of effects you prefer.

Far right, and detail, below: skilled use of stencilling creates wonderfully diverse and subtle effects, the shades melting mistily into each other with hints of the ground colour peeping through. This spectacular faux fretwork mirror and matching chest with its leopard creeping delicately through the lush foliage illustrates dramatically that stencilling can be sophisticated as well as naïve.

HAND PAINTING

Hand-painted furniture is no more difficult than stencilling, but before you begin you must let your imagination run free.

You can use anything to paint with—oils, gouaches, acrylics, water-colours, ordinary house paints, even washable or permanent felt-tip pens—it doesn't matter at all. Each medium gives a different look, each lends itself to a different style and each can be covered and protected with sprayed or brushed on varnish.

Any pattern or design can be painted—from a cheery scribble of colour to the most meticulously detailed rose. You could copy an old advertising poster on to the top of a table or toss a fake Navajo rug over a plain little chest, cover your fridge with flowers or delight your child with a farmyard bed, with lambs to count before going to sleep.

Artistic skill isn't important. Courage and imagination are, along with a careful eye for detail and the enthusiasm and determination to carry your ideas through.

Spend some time looking at paintings and decorative objects in museums and books on art to discover elements you can use. A plain wooden chair could be turned into a pointilliste fantasy, dotted all over with points of bright colour or the closely packed brushstrokes of Impressionist painting could create texture on a little chest. Loosely painted Cubist geometrics would be fun on the top of a big round table, while the more precise patterning of Middle-Eastern or Middle-European embroidery might make an exciting border for a mirror or a large chest of drawers.

Hand-painted pottery or porcelain are particularly good sources. Most have simple, quickly painted borders and motifs that can be transferred easily to furniture.

Notice the free, almost careless quality of the brush-strokes in paintings or on hand-painted pottery and china. The mistake most often made by non-professionals when painting or drawing is to try to be perfect. But the main point is to relax and enjoy what you're doing. Mistakes can always be wiped or painted away. If you've tested your ideas on waste paper before beginning, making a trial proof as when stencilling, most problems can be solved before the real work starts.

The furniture painted by Bloomsbury Group artists Duncan Grant and Vanessa Bell for their Sussex home, Charleston, was the inspiration for this old kitchen cupboard covered with still-life panels in muted pastels. Bowls of fruit and flowers, a table setting, a view of the garden are the motifs, with simple squiggles and sprays of fern forming the border.

Squiggles make the checked tablecloth, with soft blobs of colour for flowers.

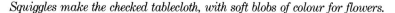

This simple kitchen chair (above) was painted glossy black and dabbed all over with bright blobs of colour. A lot more work went into the old table on the right, where the brushstrokes overlap in a shimmering kaleidoscope of colour inspired by the background of a David Hockney painting, but the basic technique—tiny patches of colour dotted on with a fine brush—is the same. The junk shop bentwood chair was painted with a bold but simple woodgrain.

Navajo Chest

The strong, geometric patterns of traditional American Indian and Indian Ikat rugs transfer easily onto painted furniture. The lines are simple and clean, the colours are either soft and muted or brilliant and bold and the repetitive designs are easily reproduced on the tops of tables or over simple chests of drawers or a blanket chest.

This plain thirties' chest was obviously mass-produced and had no charm or distinction of any kind. Found in a junk shop, it made an ideal base on which to paint a very dramatic and bold design.

Using illustrations of authentic Navajo rugs from museum catalogues and magazines, a series of sketches was drawn with felt-tip pens until a pleasing design was developed which would translate effectively in three-dimensional form. This sketch was used as the model for painting the chest.

Before beginning: The chest was prepared as described on pages 10—17, with one important difference: instead of a single base-coat of colour covering the entire piece, this coat of paint became part of the design.

Materials: Oil-based mid-sheen paint in the chosen colours; 4in (100mm) brush for each colour; gouache paint in the chosen colours; a fine camel's hair brush for sketching in the design plus 1in (25mm) camel's hair brushes, one for each colour; white spirit; clean rags or paper towelling for cleaning up; newspaper to protect the floor.

Method: The four drawers were removed from the chest. Two were painted in the darkest colour and two in the paler shade. They were replaced in the chest with the two colours alternating. These alternating bands of colour were then repeated on the top of the chest with a narrow, unpainted gap between each band. Ruled guidelines kept the bands straight and even.

The sides of the chest and frame were then painted in the third shade, which was used also in the gaps between the bands of colour on the top.

At this stage, the chest was painted in alternating bands of dark and pale colour parted by a third colour, with the third colour repeated on the sides. It was then ready for the bold pattern of bright colour and black to be zig-zagged over it.

Firstly, the design was sketched in with loose, quick lines using the fine camel's hair brush and slightly diluted black gouache paint. When the lines had dried, filling in the colour began.

To paint the bold stepping stones of bright colour which patterned the 'rug', the wider 1in (25mm) camel's hair brush was dipped into the first colour and dabbed onto the surface in loose, splodgy brushstrokes. To create this effect, the feeling should be free and easy, almost careless, with each dab of the brush laying on a generous layer of colour; this is not the time for neat filling in, with all the edges immaculate. The effect here is bold and carefree, and the little sketchy black lines drawn to indicate the design need not all be covered.

When the first colour was painted in, a clean 1in (25mm) brush was used to paint in the second colour in the same loose, swift stroke.

When all of the colours had dried, the fine camel's hair brush was used to accent the original black sketch lines, but without following the lines precisely.

Just for fun, a simple woodgrain was painted on each side of the chest, using the fine camel's hair brush and black paint. There was no attempt to make it look real; instead it was kept deliberately rough and almost coarse, in keeping with the bold, free pattern on the rest of the chest.

When the paint had dried completely, allowing a week in damp climates, the chest was sprayed with clear varnish to protect it and a piece of glass cut to fit the top. In this instance, spray varnish was chosen instead of brushed on varnish, as the gouache paint has a tendency to bleed when conventional varnish is used.

A geometric Ikat design would also be appropriate for the chest, perhaps taken from a rug you already own. Take a tracing from the rug, using large sheets of tracing paper from a graphic arts supplier. Use a photocopier to reduce in size if desired. The tracing is then taped to the chest and the design transferred by punching tiny holes with a sharpened pencil along the lines of the design, leaving a tiny dot with each punch. When the tracing is removed, clearer guidelines can be drawn lightly with a pencil, following the little dots. Any pencil marks still visible when the painting is finished can simply be erased before the piece is varnished. Once again, a rough sketch of the design should be drawn first to help establish how the geometric pattern should fall.

Cardboard keeps the paint edges sharp.

Pattern covers the drawer pulls.

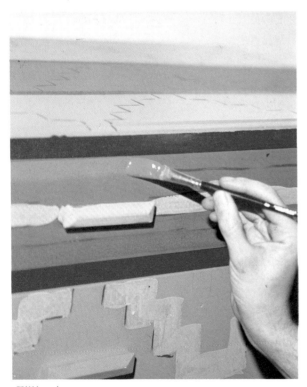
Filling in.

Woodgraining the sides.   *Opposite: the finished piece.*

Red Flower Chest

Flower painting is a favourite hobby for many people and it is just as easy to paint a bunch of daisies onto a piece of furniture as it is to paint them onto a bit of canvas. Try a bouquet of roses on the panels of a wardrobe, wind a garland of blossoms around the edge of a table or scatter a bevy of violets over a little bedside chest. You could put your flowers over a plain colour or over any of the textured surfaces already described. A pretty effect is to sponge, pounce or drag the surface in pale colour over pale and then paint one or two single blossoms, complete with stem, lying casually on the surface.

This small sideboard was painted to match a wonderful old advertising sign. By great luck, the owner found a vase in the same shape and colouring as the one in the sign and thought it would be fun to triple the image, painting a vase of flowers like the one in the picture and then filling the real vase with flowers to match.

Before beginning: The sideboard, a junk shop find, was prepared for decorating as described on pages 10—17.
Materials: Gouache paint in the desired colours; fine camel's hair brushes, one for each colour; a china saucer for each colour; paper towelling or clean rags for cleaning up; newspaper to protect the floor.
Method: A rough sketch was made first, to establish where the vase of flowers and any other decoration would be placed. Since the vase fitted best over the double doors on the base of the sideboard, it was decided to add a small bouquet on the top and tiny, matching posies on each side.

When the design was completed, the vase of flowers was roughly sketched in position, using a fine camel's hair brush and slightly diluted black gouache paint. When the sketch had dried to the touch, so that the black wouldn't bleed into the colours laid over it, the flower painting began.

Most flowers are painted easily by using a dab of the brush for each petal. Daisies are particularly easy to reproduce in this way, but violets, chrysanthemums, poppies and others can be painted quickly and simply by using one or more strokes of the brush. Shadings and highlights can be added later in darker or paler tones. Stems and leaves may be painted with the same technique, using the point of the brush for the stems and flattening the bristles for the leaves.

Every flower painter works in her or his own way, some laying on soft washes of colour while others suggest the shapes with quick strokes of brush or pen. Some work slowly and lovingly with almost photographic precision, while still others portray their blossoms impressionistically with a series of tiny

Begin by outlining the bouquet.

dots or flat flower forms. Ideas and techniques can come from gardening books or posters, from paintings or contemporary art postcards or from hand-painted pottery or porcelain. There are many excellent books on realistic flower painting; check in the local library or bookstore to find the most helpful.

Whatever technique is used, it is important to remember to sketch or draw in the shapes rather than filling them in the way one fills in the numbers in a painting kit. Colours and forms should be built up slowly, working first on one part of the picture and then on another so that the complete bouquet grows slowly before your eyes. In this way you can see how the picture is developing, whereas if you tried to finish one flower or group of blossoms completely before going on to the next, it would be much harder to balance the design.

In this case, the vase was painted very simply, building up the colour and shading slowly with quick, light brushstrokes and drawing in the pattern with short little strokes.

The bouquet on top was painted in the same manner, sketching the design in roughly with slightly thinned black and then, when the sketch had dried, painting in the flowers with quick dabs of the brush, building the shapes and shading brushstroke by brushstroke.

Finally, the posy on each side was added, again sketching in the shapes first and then building up the petals and leaves one stroke at a time.

When the paint had dried completely (allowing at least a week in damp climates) the design was protected with two coats of clear varnish, sanding down lightly after the first coat. Remember that with gouache paint, spray varnish is easier to use, especially for the first coat.

Soft and fairly realistic flowers gave this little sideboard a gentle, Victorian feeling. However, it could have been painted a bright, clear colour with simpler, more folkloric blossoms painted, in a border. Another choice would be to sponge it in muted pale colours, cream and honey, and centre the top and panels with ribbon-tied bunches of bluebells and snowdrops adding a hand-drawn line of blue around the edges. This one simple chest might have had any of three entirely different looks, each achieved with a few hand-painted flowers.

Build up the flower forms slowly, working first on one part of the picture and then on another.

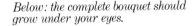

Below: the complete bouquet should grow under your eyes.

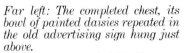

Far left: The completed chest, its bowl of painted daisies repeated in the old advertising sign hung just above.

Top left: more bright blossoms surround the memory board fridge, made with blackboard and acrylic paints with a patient cat apparently waiting for the door to open.

Top right: traditional flowers and birds cover this Victorian desk.

Below left: folkloric flowers riot over a cheerfully cluttered kitchen dresser.

Above: even a simple wooden lamp can be transformed with cheery painted flowers.

Working Out
Your Ideas

Once the right motif or design is found, the next step is to translate it into a form that can be painted easily on a table or chair. The most important thing to remember is to keep it simple. Don't try to put more than one or two ideas onto one piece of furniture, at least not in the beginning.

Perhaps you've found a plate with a pretty, hand-painted border. Using a fine camel's hair brush and gouache paint, try transferring it to a piece of paper, ruling a line to keep the border straight. If there's a simple flower or small geometric shape elsewhere in the design, pick that up and test it next to the first pattern.

When you've worked out a design that you like, use a photocopying machine to enlarge or reduce it to the size required to fit well on the chest or table. Run off several copies in different sizes to see which one works best. Planning a hand-painted design using several motifs or combinations of motifs takes the same thought and care as planning a stencilled design and laying it out on paper before beginning to paint helps to ensure that the design will work well. Run off copies of your designs on the photocopier until there are enough to complete a trial pattern. Tape each motif or piece of border onto the piece of furniture lightly and move them about until you are happy with the effect.

When you are ready to begin painting, take away each piece of test pattern and replace it with your own brushstrokes. Mark the exact shape and position of each motif with tiny pencil marks, pushing the point of a sharpened pencil through the paper along the edges of the design, making a series of dots which can be followed later. If it helps, you can always use a pin to start the little holes. Any visible pencil marks can be erased later before the piece is varnished.

Don't be afraid to take one small pattern and run it all over a chest or table without any specific form or plan. Little brightly coloured circles, tiny naive flowers, cheery hand-daubed polka dots in a bevy of colours, little clouds spaced out with stars and rainbows, small geometric or leaf forms or a combination of patterns patchworked together can all make charming decorations for mirrors or simple pieces of furniture. Combine a mixture of stripes with a naive patchwork, banding the legs and back of a chair, for example, then patchwork the seat with a hand-painted pattern, or rule a simple plaid on the top of a chest, filling in the squares with colour and striping the body in the same shades, ruling guidelines to keep the colours straight. Easiest and simplest of all, and marvellously effective in a spare, modern room, is a careless scribble of colour sprawled over the top of a table with the legs, perhaps, picking up the boldest colour in the design.

Whatever you choose, test it out on paper first, practising the technique and colouring until you are satisfied with both the look and position of the design. Then begin to paint.

Above all, relax and let your brushstrokes flow freely and easily. If you are unhappy with the way a single motif or a whole area of the design looks when it is completed, wipe it away and start again. Aim always for a light, spontaneous effect. Any tension or overcautiousness will reveal itself in the painting, making the design clumsy and uneven.

A quote from the French painter Dégas is relevant here. A patron was admiring his latest work, particularly the exquisitely painted shoe on the ballerina.

'Marvellous,' said the patron, 'just two perfect brushstrokes.'

'Yes,' said Dégas, 'and I painted it five times to get it that way.'

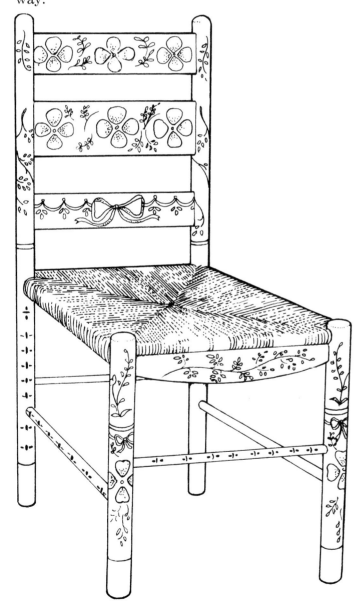

Simple flowers brushed on with little blobs of paint turn an ordinary rush-seated country chair into contemporary folk art.

Painting for Kids

Painting furniture for children is wonderful fun, mostly because they're totally uncritical as long as the subject is something they love. A junky old chest can be a London bus, a doll's house, a circus tent, a witch's cave, a pirate's ship, or even a chocolate shop. All you need to do is prop up an illustration from a favourite book, sketch in a rough design, pick up your paints and begin.

Cover the piece with one picture, like the bus or the doll's house or just add a few figures here and there—perhaps a bevy of colourfully patterned hot air balloons floating through the clouds with a few surprised birds fluttering around. A fat, white polar bear balancing a bright red ball on the end of his nose would be fun for the head of a bed, while lots of little waistcoated and petticoated mice could be hidden in odd corners of tables and chairs.

Even the simplest idea can transform a basic piece of furniture. Label the drawers of a chest 'socks, shirts, pants, sweaters,' with each letter or word (or even drawer) in a different colour. Paint a picture of the drawer's contents—a sock, a pair of trousers—on the front of each one. Make measuring a child's height more fun by painting a measuring stick up the side of a wardrobe, with alternating colours marking each new inch (or centimetre). Or have a Noah's Ark of animals around the entire room, with a pair of mice on the chair, geese on the bedside chest, elephants and giraffes on the wardrobe and the Ark itself on the bed.

Try letting the kids paint their own furniture. Bright children's drawings in permanent felt-tip pens or ordinary arcylic paints make charming decorations and wonderful family keepsakes, once protected against knocks and bangs with several coats of clear varnish.

Ordinary chipboard can be turned into magical furniture with a little paint as well. Have your local wood supplier cut a piece of chipboard in a rounded cloud shape with a hole in the middle for a mirror. Paint it white and add lots of little bright birds and flowers around the edge. A half-circle of chipboard cut and glued on top becomes a rainbow over the cloud, painted in the right cheery colours. An ordinary plain, wide-framed mirror can have a happy zig-zag of colours splashed around the edge, with brilliant little flowers centred in the middle of each triangle. A cheap and cheerful headboard for a child's bed can be made with a rectangle cut to fit. Painted a clear colour with a band of bright around the edge embellished with freely painted hearts and flowers, it can be centred with a fairyland castle, an elf's hut or a funny clown.

Top left: this plain play table became an educational toy when the top was covered with blackboard paint and the alphabet run around the edge.
Top right: any small girl would be enchanted by this doll's house chest of drawers with little animals peeping out of its windows.
Below left: a London bus chest could travel anywhere in the world.

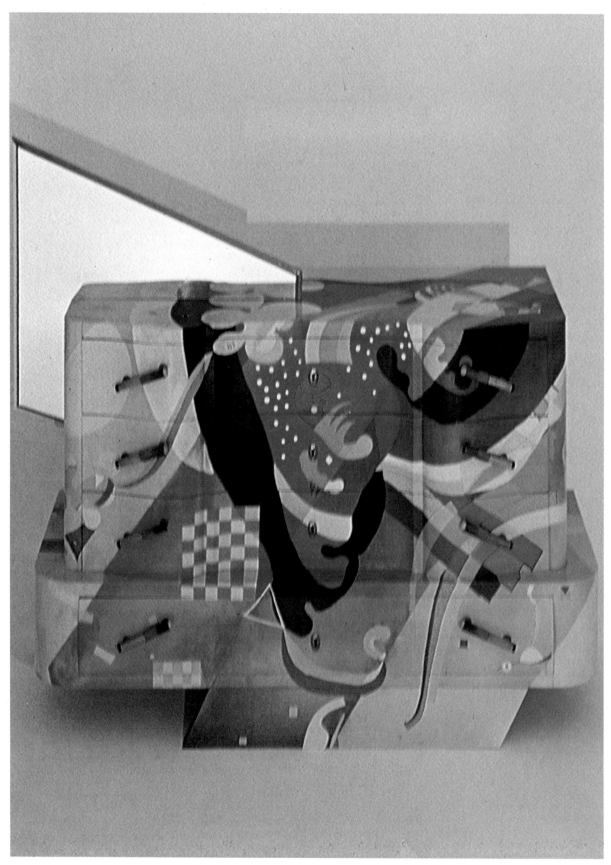

This is Italian fantasy at its most exuberant.
Far left and below: extravagant neo-Cubist painting transforms once ungainly thirties' chests of drawers.
Near left: joyous shadowed stripes swoop across basic cupboards and ornamental shelves.

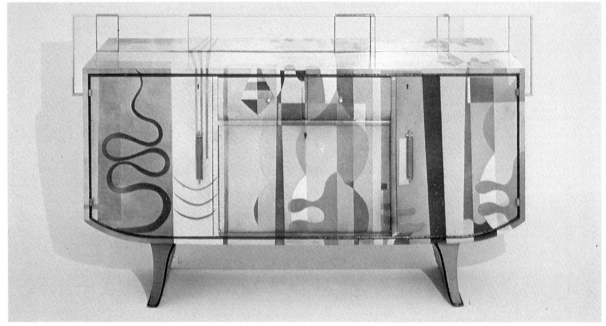

Fantasy
Furniture

Every once in a while an extraordinary breakthrough in design sends a shock wave of excitement around the world.

Sometimes it is in fashion, as when Dior's New Look or Courrège's Space Age minis captured the international imagination. Sometimes it is in architecture, as with the soaring structures of Saarinen.

It may be in industrial design, as when the stark simplicity of matt black high tech invaded everything from fountain pens to portable radios. At the moment the breakthrough is in furnishings, with the uninhibited decorative fantasies of the Italian avant garde creating an explosion of imaginatively coloured and patterned furniture which defies all previous ideas of good design.

This 'Post Modernist' style has become strongly identified with the Milan group, Memphis, who are in revolt against the stark, strictly functional Modern Movement which has dominated architecture, art and industrial design since the 1920s. The new movement is one of aesthetic anarchy. There are no rules and good taste has been discarded along with 'clean lines', 'truth to materials', 'unity of style', and all of the other 'less is more' principles of Modernism.

The new images are drawn from everywhere—from the fifties, from classical architecture, from science fiction, from Cubist, Surrealist and Pointilliste art and from fashion. The designers say that they are trying to discover 'the lost grace of the applied arts', using colour and decoration as both a game and ornament. The decoration is achieved not by going back to traditional craft techniques and processes, but through the most progressive industrial technology, using plastic laminates, silkscreen prints, collage (or découpage) and the unexpected juxtapositioning of precious and non-precious materials and unrelated surfaces such as wood, plastic, glass, marble and fabrics.

To the observer, the most immediate impact is in the riotous colour, shape and patterning of the new pieces. The furniture all functions in that you can still sit on it or eat off of it, but rarely does it conform to any established idea of a chair or a table. Even if it does, there is always at least one joyously discordant element that brings a sharp shock of surprise like a fifties-style chair beautifully faux marbled, or the narrow, eight-drawer chest with its army camouflage-patterned frame, square feet, and drawer handles like a robot's antennae.

Many of these avant garde experiments have been on authentic fifties' or thirties' furniture, and its bold, anarchistic designs offer the most amusing and original treatment for junk shop finds that might otherwise be disregarded. The free mixture of patterns can be imitated with découpage and paint, and the resulting dramatic and lighthearted pieces add an off-beat accent to any setting.

Doing It Yourself

The key to a successful Post Modernist look is excess: do nothing in moderation. You have a much hated batch of battered chrome and plastic kitchen chairs? Marvellous! Cover them in the most inappropriate finish you can think of. Why not brilliantly coloured fake marble? And if you have old Formica kitchen cabinets, you could paint them in radiating bands of red, blue and yellow marble.

Even easier to accomplish are the Pointilliste effects, with every available inch of the chest covered with tiny, vibrantly coloured, overlapping blobs of paint. The blobs can be tiny or huge, round or roughly squarish. You could make them out of loosely cut paper, using tissue paper in pale or bright colours cut at random and pasted on in merry abandon. Try mixing geometrically patterned gift-wrapping paper with solid colour or, even better, using several patterns all together. Swirling, free-wheeling geometric shapes are a major element of Post Modernist design. Busy-ness is the key.

Colour is important. Post Modernist colours are vivid and intense, with surprising contrasts similar to those seen in avant garde fashion. Baby pink and baby blue sharpened with black; pale peach and black mated with red, white and blue; or saffron yellow paired with electric blue, soft peach and mauve. Once again, it is the off-beat, unexpected element which gives that essential shiver of excitement.

Post Modernist decoration can be used on any style or period of furniture and it is this often deliberate juxtaposition of old and new that creates much of the effect. Stolid thirties' sideboards or bland fifties' and sixties' commercial furniture take on an aura of magic once given this fanciful treatment.

Tiny, cleanly cut rectangles and curving, amoeba-like shapes are sent whirling over the surface in this design for an interior.

DECOUPAGE

Découpage decoration is really no different from the sticky paper pictures made by children. Just cut out simple shapes from plain paper or pretty pictures from a magazine or printed fabric or paper and glue them down in any combination that pleases.

Découpage can be big and bold or delicate and charming, cover an object completely or form a spaced-out pattern with the ground colour showing through.

Matisse was the great master of découpage, with almost all of the work of his later years created in this medium. Brightly coloured curving shapes are mixed in vibrant combinations, at once sophisticated and naive. Much in the same mood are the appliqué quilts of nineteenth-century Hawaii, where intricately cut, whirling forms are set in bright colour on bright.

Victorian ladies worked with découpage, too, gluing pretty little pictures onto boxes and screens and even on the insides of giant glass bottles. Later, in the twenties and thirties, Cubist and Futurist artists used découpage combined with paint to create the shimmering images that were the focus of their work.

Découpage can be expanded beyond the creation of flat patterns. Add coloured mouldings, ridged and fluted columns, plaster or plastic coated fabric, vinyl or Formica, bits of mirror or broken china or anything else which satisfies the creative eye. There are obvious practical difficulties, however, and you would need to be prepared to give your work extra care and attention in relation to the materials you have used.

Here, therefore, we have concentrated on the simplest and most enjoyable aspect of découpage, creating smooth, happy images by the quickest and most durable means.

Left: this intricately pieced table is assembled easily with sticky-backed plain shelf lining paper. The design is in squares, measured and marked on the surface with a fine pencilled line. The bright blue and navy lining papers were then cut into squares of the measured size, enough to cover the table top. When ready, most were re-cut into sticks and rectangles, triangles and squares, fish scales and floppy forms inspired by the work of Matisse. With the sticky backing in place, the cut out shapes were placed on the table inside the pencilled squares and shifted about, mixing colours and shapes, until a pleasing pattern was formed. With the pieces in position, each was picked up, stripped of its sticky backing and replaced until the pattern was completed.

Decorated Filing Cabinet

Almost any simple design in flat colours can be used as the basis for a construction paper découpage. The pattern (page 106) was taken from an old English quilt, but a picture by Matisse, a child's drawing, striped deck chair canvas or a contemporary art postcard would be equally good as sources. The main point is to keep it simple.

The piece itself must be simple as well. A filing cabinet is ideal, but kitchen cabinets, or a cheap chest of drawers would be equally as good. This kind of flat applied pattern will not work on a table with a lot of drawers or details.

Materials: Red and blue construction paper (the largest sheets available); a can of artist's spray adhesive; scissors; rubbing alcohol or rubber cement thinner. You can use ordinary brush-on glue (preferably of the kind produced for professional artists), but it is messier and more difficult to control. Spray adhesive gives exactly the right amount of stickiness to the surface, and allows you to reposition the decoration if necessary. When the work is complete, any excess glue is cleaned off with alcohol or rubber cement thinner.

Beginning: Each side of the white painted filing cabinet was carefully measured and two inches of plain white were left at the top and bottom of the cabinet to create a perfect square—24x24in (600x600mm). This was then divided into four 2in (50mm) bands of colour with an 8in (220mm) centre panel. For the borders, four 2x20in (50x200mm) and four 2x8in (50x200mm) strips of blue paper were cut plus four 2in by 16in (50x400mm) strips of red paper.

The strip of blue paper which formed the top border was pasted down 2in (50mm) from the top and 2in (50mm) in from either side. In order to place it correctly a ruler was used to make two tiny pencil marks 2in (50mm) below the top of the cabinet and, at the same level, 2in (50mm) in from each side. The paper stripe was then sprayed lightly (on the wrong or reverse side) with adhesive and—having been held for a second or two to allow the adhesive to get tacky—was pressed firmly into place and smoothed by the palm of the hand. If, at this point, the paper isn't placed correctly, it's easy to lift it off and replace it, using the pencil marks to correct the position.

This procedure was repeated with the other strips, leaving 2in (50mm) squares of white paint exposed at each corner. The same method was used for the inner border—using the edge of the first border to place the pencil marks. The white border was created by leaving a 2in (50mm) gap between the red border and the innermost blue border.

The large motif in the centre and the corner motifs were

made by folding small pieces of paper and cutting them in the same way that a lace paper doiley is cut out. The corner motifs were cut from two inch squares and the centre motif from an 8in (200mm) square. (A little experimentation will give you the knack very quickly and there are almost endless shapes that can be created.) The motifs were applied in the same way as the borders. The motif was sprayed with adhesive, held a second or two to get tacky, and then smoothed down.

The top and front of the filing cabinet are variations on the master design in the same way that the patch patterns in a quilt were often variations on a theme. The cut-out shapes can be played with freely. As long as they're kept simple, almost any combination of designs will work.

To finish: When the applied decoration on all sides of the cabinet was completed, excess adhesive was cleaned off with alcohol or rubber cement thinner, according to the directions on the can. The découpage was then protected with two coats of clear polyurethane varnish, rubbed down with fine sandpaper between each coat, and a piece of bevelled edge glass was cut to fit the top.

Top: single folds are cut into simple heart and flower shapes.
Centre: double folding into rectangle and then square shapes permit cut-out centres.
Bottom: folding a square into ever smaller triangles allows for elaborate star shapes.

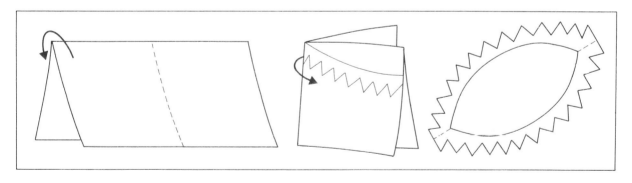

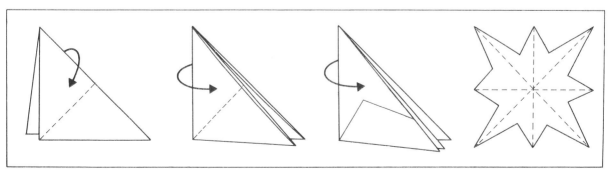

106

Left: flowers cut out of a garden catalogue are prettily découpaged onto a little pine cabinet.

Far left: completed patchwork découpage filing cab:net adds a delightful accent to a kitchen or playroom.

Below: more ideas for cutouts can come from Indian or Middle Eastern and Middle European folk art.

Torn Paper
Screen

Even quicker and easier than cutting out shapes from coloured paper is tearing them out—making rough, almost abstract forms which can be glued together to represent flowers, leaves, trees, latticework, grass, animals, houses, or anything else. Use tissue paper, newspaper, construction paper, gift wrapping paper, hand-made papers, or almost any other kind of paper, either each on its own or combined with two or more other types of paper. The only papers which might cause problems are metallics; the shiny surface makes it difficult for the protective coating of varnish to adhere properly.

Pattern your own paper before tearing it; tie and dye plain white paper napkins or any other fairly sturdy but absorbent papers by simply screwing them up and dipping them into cold water fabric dye or diluted acrylic or gouache paints (or even tea or coffee), carefully opening them up immediately, then ironing flat and dry. (Cover the board with an old towel or paper towelling that can be thrown away later.) Paint little patterns with felt-tips or drawing inks, tearing the paper into patches or borders for the main designs. Even little bits of ribbon or brightly coloured thread can be trailed across the torn paper, and fixed with spray adhesive; the soft, random look fits in nicely with the ragged edges. The thread or ribbon leaves a slight texture on the surface, even after varnishing, but this doesn't really matter.

Making the Screen
This six-fold screen was made easily and swiftly using pre-cut panels of plywood hinged together with brass. It was painted white and then decorated with a flower-covered lattice of torn tissue paper.

Left: the border pieces are torn out of straight strips of tissue paper. Right: the flower forms are torn in rounded shapes.

Materials: 6 panels of ½in (12mm) thick plywood, each measuring 54 x 11 in (135 x 27.5cm); 10 brass hinges with nails; flat oil-based paint; tissue paper in bright pink, yellow, orange, blue, green and black; artist's spray adhesive (available in art supply shops). Wallpaper paste can be substituted, but it is messier and less easy to use.

Before beginning: The panels were bought cut to order and laid out on newspaper on the floor in the form of a six-fold screen. After sanding, they were painted white (flat, in this instance, as durability was not important, but mid-sheen would have done as well) on both sides and left to dry for 24 hours.

Method: The wide black border was torn and pasted first, with all six panels seen as one, unified whole. To make the border, strips of paper about 2—3in (50—75mm) wide were torn off the straight edge of the black tissue paper and glued onto the edge of the screen. The strips were attached using artist's spray adhesive, spraying the reverse or wrong side of the strip of paper lightly, allowing it to dry for a few seconds, and then pressing it into position at the edge of the screen, with one edge slightly overlapping the end of the previous strip. As tissue paper is slightly transparent, there is a deepening of colour where the edges overlap, creating a stained glass effect. (If you do not like this look, substitute opaque construction paper.)

When the black frame was complete, the big, pink flower shapes were torn and pasted. These were soft, irregular pieces of tissue paper torn with no attempt to make them follow any real flower outline, but giving the idea of flower by colour and form. These were spaced out at random over the entire white area in a casual, impromptu manner.

The other colours were then added slowly, torn in various sizes and shapes, and scattered out over the entire design, sometimes overlapping with the longer, narrower leaf shapes scattered in between. When the pattern of leaves and flowers was completed, the fine black latticework was added. Very narrow strips of black were torn out of the left-over black tissue

Below left and centre: when the border is complete, the flower forms are added one by one, building the design one colour at a time.
Below right: when the design is finished, the panels are hinged together.

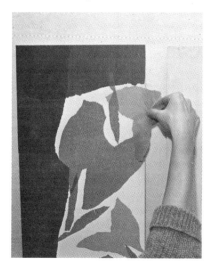 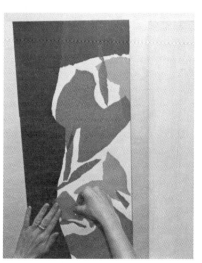 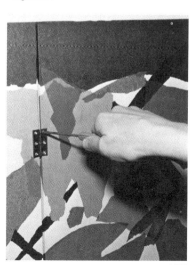

paper and glued in place in a delicate criss-crossing design. When the lattice reached a blossom or leaf, the black tissue paper was simply torn off and continued on the other side of the flower. Occasionally it was allowed to cover a flower, as though the blossom had slipped through the lattice to the other side.

Looseness and irregularity is what gives this piece much of its vibrancy; they stem directly from the torn paper

technique. More careful or more even tearing would spoil most of the screen's charm.

When the design was completed, the panels were protected with a coat of clear varnish which was allowed to dry for twenty-four hours. The panels were then hinged together to make a six-fold screen, alternating the hinged sides from front to back and front again, allowing the screen to stand firmly.

The completed screen, dramatic enough to work like a painting, as the focal point of a simple room.

Striping

Striping is an easy way to give a crisp and professional finish to a simply textured piece of furniture or to add an air of drama and importance to a piece that is very plain. Like the frame of a painting, the lines can be delicate and soft or bright and bold and the choice of style depends only on the shape of the piece and the desired effect.

The most basic use of striping is to outline the top of a table or chest or frame the drawers or legs and the difference made by a few simple lines of colour can be amazing. A small, undistinguished table will take on importance, a boring chest gain distinction, and even an unwieldy piece of furniture can be brought into proportion and given a new strength and style.

Basic striping can be used by itself on a plain painted surface or over almost any painted texture, or it can be used in combination with stencilling or hand painting, with or without a painted texture decorative technique. Interior decorators often add a hand-painted stripe of colour to simple, dragged or sponged tables or chests of drawers, or frame the panels of a wardrobe which may first have been sponged and painted with flowers. Traditionalists use the most subtle stripings, often simply a darker shade of the ground or texturing colours. Sometimes this can be very pretty, as the bedroom chests painted cream, sponged with rose pink and then striped with darker pink. Other colours give an antiqued effect, as the reproduction Chippendale shelves painted pale green, dragged with deeper green and then striped with a fine line of green muted with grey.

Excitement comes with sharper combinations such as bright blue striped on spattered blue, yellow and green on white, or leafy green striped on pale yellow.

Striping can be used as a decorative technique in itself. An absolutely plain modern chipboard chest could be painted white and banded with parallel stripes of red and blue for a little boy's room, or plaided with criss-cross bands of pale pink and blue to match the ribbons in a little girl's hair.

Masked Striping

The fastest form of striping is also the simplest—a broad, straight band masked either side with tape and coloured by sponging or brushing on. It is important, however, to test both colour and position on paper before starting, transferring the plan to the piece of furniture in chalk to make sure the design is satisfactory. Once this is done, it is time to begin.

Materials: A 1in (25mm) brush; 1in (25mm) masking tape; oil-based paint thinned with white spirit; white spirit; rags.

Above: painting on the masked-off stripe.
Below: removing the masking tape.

112

Method: With a tape measure, carefully measure the position and width of each band, marking them in pencil. Place the masking tape carefully in position, and press it down hard, running your fingers firmly along the entire length. The tape should completely frame the area to be striped.

Dip the brush or sponge in the thinned paint and colour the stripe quickly and lightly. Leave the tape in place for a few minutes, until the paint has touch dried, and then remove. Any blobs which have flowed under the tape can be wiped away with white spirit, using a rag wrapped tightly around one finger and dipped in the fluid.

This process will give a clean, clear line of colour, but if a faded or worn look is desired, simply rub here and there with the finest grade of sandpaper or wire wool as soon as the paint is dry.

Hand-painted Striping

Hand-painted striping is simple to do with a steady hand and confidence. Any hesitation, unfortunately, will show. A fine camel's hair artist's brush is used, its delicacy depending on the fineness of the line desired. The brush is filled with paint and any excess tapped off. Keeping the arm and hand relaxed, stand far enough away from the piece to allow the shoulder and arm free play when striping. As the brush is pulled along, watch a point slightly ahead of the brush and a clean, straight line should be produced. Hold the brush well up the handle and away from the bristles. The longer the length of handle between fingers and brush, the longer and freer the sweep of line. If there is a bit of nervous wobble, *do not* lift the brush away; keep on going. A slight unevenness in the line will look fine in the end, but if you lift the brush and try to correct a little flutter, it will spoil the continuity. If the line really looks terrible, wipe the entire length away with white spirit and begin again. Any small slip or blob of paint can be wiped away with white spirit too.

Guided Striping

A clean edge can be used as a convenient guide for striping. Lean the brush at a 45° angle against the edge and move it down to mark the line. To fill in, run the brush along the line.

Artists' supply shops sell a variety of simple instruments to help professionals draw curves and lines of varying kinds. A little investigation should produce several useful tools. You can make your own guide, too, by notching a piece of cardboard. If you wish a stripe round a table to be 2in (50mm) from the edge, for example, make the notch 2in (50mm) deep. Then place the edge of the cardboard on the edge of the table and mark the point of the notch with a pencil or brush. Go round the edge of the table marking the points at intervals; this should leave a line of marks which can be followed to paint a stripe. When painting, support the wrist with the other hand or by resting the elbow against a handy surface to keep the line steady, but make sure the pressure is constant and keep moving!

IDEAS

Almost any material can be used in découpage: brightly coloured and patterned cut-outs from magazines, flower catalogues, gift wrapping paper, comic books or printed fabrics or freshly created patterns cut out of coloured construction paper, tissue paper, sticky shelf paper or even the little bits of brightly coloured paper sold for children to use in making pictures. Ordinary sheets of coloured writing paper can be overlapped to create abstracts, or cut out giant circles and rectangles from plain paper and glue them one over the other in imitation of abstract and minimalist paintings. Small and larger squares can be spaced out neatly to make intricately constructed pictures in the way that a child creates elaborate constructions out of little blocks of Lego. Even a group of

randomly cut geometric shapes from ordinary coloured paper can be scattered casually to make dramatic designs.

What counts once again is courage and imagination. Look for ideas everywhere, in abstract paintings, patchwork quilts, the bold geometrics of African and Amerindian art and the Middle East, and the bright and happy folk-art of Sweden and Denmark. What you need are strong, simple forms which can be cut out of plain paper or smaller, pretty designs which can be cut out of already patterned paper or fabric and combined in new and interesting ways.

If you can't find the patterns you want, there's no reason why you shouldn't create your own. Use felt-tip pens on plain paper to make the geometrics or flowers which will give the look you need.

Remember that lighter weight papers and fabrics will be easier to work with. The spray mount adhesive makes even the most delicate tissue paper easy to handle. If you prefer to work with brushed on glue, be sure to use the smallest possible amount needed to smooth down your work. The protective coat of varnish will hold them down firmly.

Far left: it's fun to tell a story with découpage. The panelled wardrobe, has its owner with her cat gazing at the starry night sky.
Centre top: the toy chest is covered with gay comic strip posters, completed with ballooned conversation.
Centre below: a cut-out goose tugs its mistress around the corner of this chest of drawers.
Right: more sophisticated, but just as lighthearted, the four-fold screen with cut-out fruit and palm trees in a tropical mood.

Imaginative decorating transforms even the most prosaic object.
Far left: a curving vine, painted with the help of a home-made cardboard curve, can border an old wardrobe or chest of drawers or run around the edge of a table.
Centre left: a wall of cabinets becomes lighter and gayer when each panel is painted with latticework and centred with a découpaged page from an old flower calendar.
Above left: ordinary little baskets are fun covered with bright diamonds and zig-zags.
Below: even a simple home-made wooden screen is easily and dramatically striped with bands of colour scribbled on with thick felt-tip pens.

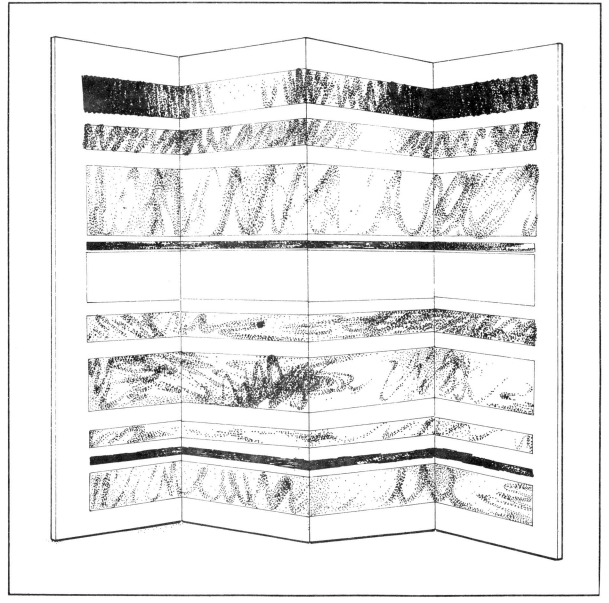

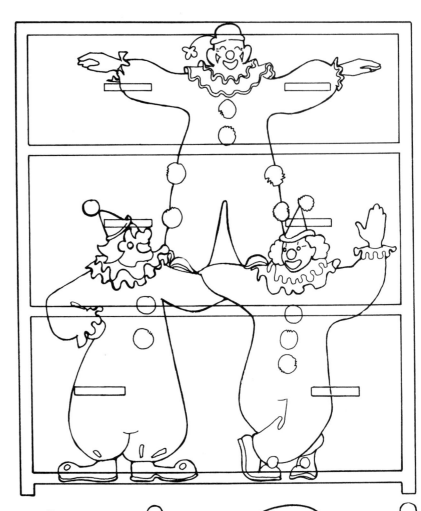

Simple, brightly coloured figures can be cut out of tissue or construction paper and découpaged onto a chest or bed or painted on with ordinary household paint tinted to the shade needed. Right: a clown pyramid makes a bit of fun out of a basic chest of drawers. Below: a favourite nursery rhyme covers the end of a baby's cot.

Left: a patchwork of scribbly flowers painted on with felt tip pens or
artist's acrylics turns a plain
modern frame into something very
personal. Below: a painted break-
fast tray complete with sugar bowl
and coffee cup lets everyone know
what's inside that particular set of
kitchen cabinets. Wobbly, hand-
drawn lines add to its charm.

FUNDAMENTALS

Paint is composed of a *vehicle* holding everything together, *pigments* which give colour, opacity and body, and *thinners* which bring the mixture to a spreading consistency. There is a wide variety of paints available for covering walls, furniture, floors, cement, brick and other surfaces, but here we are concerned with paints suitable for furniture alone.

The Base Coat
Apart from colour and finish, durability is of prime importance. Tables, chairs and other items in daily use are banged and knocked against as part of normal wear and tear and for this reason, professionals tend to use alkyd (oil-based) paints for furniture as they are extremely tough. Traditionally, such paints were based on linseed oil which dries to form a solid paint film. Today, the linseed has been largely replaced by the better synthetic resins called alkyds. These paints come in matt, mid-sheen (also called semi-sheen, silk or satin) or high gloss finishes. (These are termed velvet, eggshell, low-lustre or satin finish in ascending order of shine in the US.) In decorating furniture, the mid-sheen finish is preferred to the matt or high-gloss as it holds the decorative finish well and gives a nice, porcelain-like surface for the decoration to work against.

Polyurethane (oil-based) paints: These contain polyurethane binders or urethane-modified alkyd. Most of these—particularly the glosses—are thixotropic; they are jellylike in the can, but become liquid when shaken or stirred and are less likely to drip than other types.

Both alkyd and polyurethane oil-based paints are thinned with white spirit.

Emulsion (water-based) paints: These are not recommended for furniture for two important reasons; they are not as durable as oil-based paints (although this is to some degree overcome with a protective coating of polyurethane varnish) and the more absorbent surfaces gives a less clean and crisp finish to most decorative techniques. There is one exception to this rule, however; flat emulsion has the same, chalky look as the old lead-based paints used on many country pieces. A single coat of sludgy red, blue or green roughly painted over bare and lightly sanded wood gives the right coarse look, especially if some of the paint is wiped off, simulating wear, before it has dried. Any decoration can be added with acrylic paints and a protective coating of matt polyurethane varnish laid on top. Durability doesn't really matter here, as the daily nicks and gouges simply enhance the illusion of age.

When the base coat of paint is completely dry—which can take up to a week in damp climates— it is then ready for decoration to be applied.

Decoration
In deciding which medium to use for texturing, hand-painting, stencilling, etc., there is a lot of flexibility.

Alkyd (oil-based) paints: These are used straight from the tin for stencilling, spattering or hand-painting. The thick consistency is an advantage, especially in stencilling, and can be thinned with white spirit when necessary. Small amounts are easily coloured to your needs using tinting colours (universal stainers, tinters) which come in a range of basic colours, or with artists' oil paints which are more expensive, but offer a wide choice of colours and are convenient if you are uncertain of your ability to match a colour or simply don't want to bother.

To mix a specific colour, it is easiest to start with plain white, although a pale shade in the colour family you are using (for instance, shell pink if you want something in the red/orange/purple/pink range) is fine, too. Only a small amount of paint is needed for most decorating, so put no more than six to eight tablespoons (roughly half a tea cup full) of paint into a glass jar and add tinter or oil paint a few drops at a time, stirring thoroughly after each addition and testing a bit on a sheet of paper, until you arrive at the desired colour. Screw the top back onto the jar to keep the paint from forming a skin until you are ready to proceed.

Alkyd or polyurethane (oil-based) paints: These can be conveniently used for decorative texturing effects as well, although the look will be less translucent than glazes. Simply thin down with white spirit, starting with equal parts of paint and solvent and then adding more white spirit until you reach a satisfactory texture. Thinned oil-based paint dries more quickly than specially made glazes and thus is more difficult for beginners to use on large areas such as walls, but in furniture you are working so quickly, anyway, that the faster drying time really doesn't matter. If the mixture becomes too thin to texture properly, try adding a little drier (available at specialist or trade paint suppliers) at the rate of one teaspoon to the half-litre (one US pint).

Glaze: Called 'scumble glaze' in Britain, glazing liquid or glaze coat in the US). This is a ready-made base needing only an addition of colour mixed in the same manner as the oil-based paints described above. Proprietary glaze is convenient and easy to use, as it is designed to remain workable and wet long enough for decorative effects to be finished easily. Depending on the brand, transparent glazes can be anything from thick and golden, like a jellied honey, down to a thinned white cream which, when brushed out and allowed to dry, turns transparent. Glaze dries to a slight sheen and can be used for most decorative effects. It yellows slightly with time, but this generally enhances the warm, mellowed look. It's certainly the easiest medium for beginners to use and is preferred by professionals as well. Glazes can be thinned with white spirit to increase their spreading capacity. Thinned down to a watery consistency, glazes make a beautifully clear wash for colourwashing.

As ready-made glazes can be difficult to find, it seems sensible to include a recipe for a home-made glaze which, while definitely not as satisfactory as the proprietary glazes, can be useful. Mix equal parts of boiled linseed oil and white spirit and add a small amount—two or three tablespoons—of drier (available in trade and speciality paint suppliers), and tint to whatever colour is desired. Be careful not to add too much drier, as the colour is quite dark and, with the amber of the linseed oil, makes it difficult to reach the clear, pure shades which are preferred. This mixture takes several days to dry, due to the high proportion of linseed oil, but can give pleasing results if carefully used.

An easier alternative is mid-sheen interior wood varnish tinted with oil-based tinters or artists' oil paints and thinned slightly with white spirit if necessary. While varnish (especially the modern, quick-drying polyurethane varnish) is not an acceptable alternative to proprietary glaze for walls or any other large surfaces as it will not stay wet and workable for very long, it is perfectly fine for small areas. Since only one part of a piece of furniture is textured at a time—such as the drawers of a chest or the top of a table—each section is finished well before the varnish dries. However, be sure to varnish the complete section on which you are working—that is the whole side of the chest or the entire front of the drawer, and not just part of it, or else you will create an edge which is difficult to blend when you go back to work on the rest of the section.

Tips for Different Techniques

Hand painting and spattering both allow a great deal of flexibility in the types of paint which can be used. For spattering, drawing inks give a wonderfully translucent quality, allowing you to splash and spatter far more roughly than with opaque paints and still achieve delightfully intricate effects, particularly with delicate pastels overlapping one another. Thinned artists' oil paints, gouache or acrylics are other excellent alternatives, each offering a wide choice of colour. For hand painting use any and all of these alternatives, plus permanent felt-tip pens which also give a wide colour choice and a pleasing transluscence. With felt-tips, you can even find day-glo colours, fun for a child's or teenager's room.

Try felt-tips for stencilling, as well, working in a series of closely packed dots. Also try stencilling with the thickest brand of proprietary scumble glaze, laying one stencil over the other for a delicately transparent overlapping of colour.

Spray paints for artists' use expand the range of possibilities even further, They can be used for stencilling or in combination with texturing or hand-painted techniques, laying on an airy cloud of colour above or below another texture or pattern. A warning: do not be tempted to use car retouching sprays. Most are made with cellulose solvents which can attack alkyd paints. Better be safe than risk spoiling all your careful work.

The Protective Finish
Clear polyurethane varnish: This gives a tough, protective coating to a decorated piece. Be sure to buy the clearest available, as some have a pronounced yellowish tinge which can drastically alter your own choice of colour. A little yellowing is inevitable, adding warmth and mellowness to most finishes.

Matt varnish: This dries with no shine and is almost invisible. It works well on simple, rustic pieces, especially where the paint and wood is rough and uneven.

Semi-gloss or silk finish varnish: This is generally the most useful; it gives a nice, soft glow that enhances most decorative techniques.

Gloss varnish: This is the toughest and most durable but also the most demanding as it shows up every bit of unevenness in the surface. Use gloss for small pieces that get a lot of wear, like trays or boxes, and rub it down lightly with the finest wire wool if the shine seems too harsh.

Method: To apply varnish, work in a warm (70°F or 20°C) room with plenty of fresh air, but no draughts. Fresh air helps the varnish dry, but spreads the smell around the house. Make sure that you put plenty of slightly dampened (to reduce dust) newspaper under the piece and cover yourself up well to keep the varnish off your clothes.

Buy a good, thick, soft varnish brush, with a chisel-like edge—or at least the best brush you can find—and keep it for varnishing only.

Always buy a good varnish, as cheap ones tend to crack and peel. When the tin is opened, the varnish should be thin enough to brush on easily, without any pulling or sticking. If necessary, it can be made more fluid by sitting the tin in warm water for ten minutes or by adding a few drops of the recommended solvent (see brand label for details). It is necessary to stir matt or satin varnish, as many brands tend to settle after standing. Never stir gloss varnish, however, as the ingredients do not settle and motion can cause bubbles. Wiping the brush against the side of the tin causes bubbles, too; press the bristles gently against the side of the tin instead.

Brush varnish in one direction only, loading the brush halfway up the bristles and moving quickly and carefully. Start in the centre of the piece and spread the varnish out to the sides, going over the first strokes to smooth any gaps and break any bubbles which may have formed. Flick out any hairs, grit or bits of fluff with the edge of the brush or a darning needle, and smooth over immediately.

Leave the freshly varnished piece to dry in a warm, dry room for at least twenty-four hours and varnish again. Sand lightly before applying the third and subsequent coats.

123

Coloured varnishes throw an extra transparent gleam of colour over the entire decorative scheme. There is a generous range of shades available in commercially shaded varnishes or tint your own with oil-based stainers or artist's oil paints in the same way as for decorative glazes.

Tinted varnishes are particularly effective when used over other transparent decorative techniques, for example, over glazes, over permanent felt-tip pen drawings or over tissue paper découpage. Brush on a single coat of tinted varnish and then rub it down lightly with the finest grade of wire wool, wiping it clean and waxing for a subtle, gleaming look, or lay one coat of tinted varnish over another for a deeper, more intense glow. Finally, brush on one or two coats of tinted varnish until the desired depth of colour is reached and then layer two or more coats of clear gloss varnish on top for a rich, lacquered look.

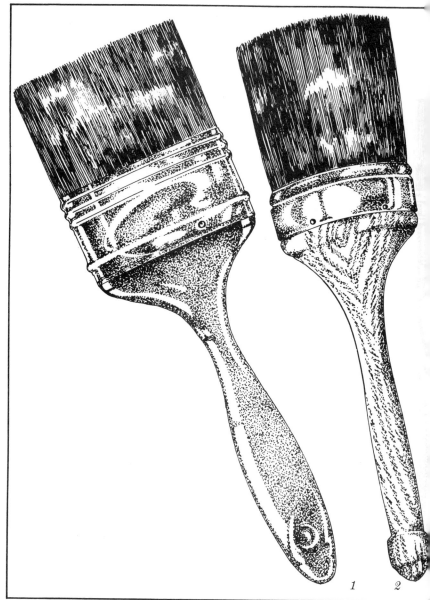

Basic brushes: (1) for furniture, a medium-sized brush, between 50 and 75mm (2 and 3 in) wide is best. (2) a special oval varnishing brush between 25 and 75mm (1 and 3 in) should be kept for varnishing only. (3) a small brush, 25mm (1 in) or narrower, is handy for fiddly bits like legs and chair rungs. (4) artist's brushes are needed for hand-painting and lining. The most useful are the soft-bristled type (sable or camel's hair) with a tapering point and the shorter handled, water-colour brushes are easiest to use. As you become more skilled, you may find that particular brushes are best for certain details—thinner brushes for fine lining and fatter brushes for simple blossoms. (5) Lining brushes with wedge-cut bristles are worth finding as they do make lining borders along a straight edge much easier. (6) Stencil brushes come in several sizes, from 6 to 50mm ($^1_4$ to 2 in) across. Smaller ones are best for tiny, fiddly stencils while the bigger ones, obviously, cover large areas more quickly. A cut-off, straight-edged small painting brush or hog's hair artist's brush will do at a pinch, as long as the bristles are firm and flat.

1   2

Table Tops

The tops of tables, bedside chests or any other surfaces which are likely to have cups of hot beverages, or other drinks put on them should be given extra protection. Paint, even when protected with several coats of polyurethane varnish, can be marred or ringed by alcohol or hot drinks in the same way as fine wax or french polished surfaces. If a table or chest top is intended for heavy use, protect it completely with a piece of plastic or top-weight glass cut to fit (with the edges bevelled for safety). Glass is usually the best choice, especially for table tops which will get a lot of wear, as it is both hard and durable. If the surface is to be used by children or is flexible in any way (as, for example, a large desk top made out of chipboard and resting on filing cabinets), plastic is the better choice, although it scratches more easily. It is also much lighter in weight and, of course, unbreakable.

3   4   5   6

Recommended Reading

These are some of the books you may find helpful in researching ideas for transforming furniture.

Adams, Janet Woodbury. **Decorative Folding Screens.** *Thames & Hudson, London 1982.*

Anscombe, Isabelle. **Omega and after, Bloomsbury and the Decorative Arts.** *Thames & Hudson, London 1981.*

Aragon, Louis (Translated by Jean Stewart). **Henri Matisse.** *William Collins and Sons, London 1972.*

Bakst Leon. (Translated by Harry Melville). **The Decorative Art of Leon Bakst.** *Constable and Co, London 1972; Dover Publications Inc, New York, 1972.*

Betterton, Sheila. **Quilts and Coverlets.** *The American Museum in Britain, Bath, 1978.*

Bishop, Adele and Lord, Cile. **The Art of Decorative Stencilling.** *Thames & Hudson Ltd, London 1976; Viking Press Inc, New York, 1976.*

Chapman, Suzanne E. **Early American Design Motifs.** *Dover Publications Inc, New York 1974.*

Colby, Averil. **Patchwork.** *B.T. Batsford Ltd, London 1958*

Delaunay, Sonia. **Rhythms and Colours.** *Thames & Hudson, London 1972; Hermann, Paris 1971.*

Feder, Norman. **American Indian Art.** *Harry N. Abrams Inc, New York 1970.*

Foley, Edwin. **The Book of Decorative Furniture, Vols 1 and 2.** *T.C. & E.C. Jack Ltd, London and Edinburgh.*

Hansen, H.J. (Ed). **European Folk Art.** *Thames & Hudson Ltd, London 1968.*

Healey, Deryck. **Living with Colour.** *Macmillan, London 1982.*

Innes, Jocasta. **Paint Magic.** *Windward/Berger Paints, London 1981; USA 1981*

Kahlenberg, Mary Hunt & Berlant, Anthony. **The Navajo Blanket.** *Praeger Publishers Inc, Los Angeles, California 1972.*

Kettell, Russell Hawes. **Early American Rooms 1650-1858.** *Dover Publications Inc, New York 1967.*

Lenclos, Jean Philippe and Lenclos, Dominique. **Les Couleurs de la France Maisons et paysages.** *Moniteur, Paris 1982.*

Lipman, Jean. **American Folk Decoration.** *Dover Publications Inc, New York 1972.*

Lipman, Jean & Winchester, Alice. **The Flowering of American Folk Art.** *The Viking Press Inc, New York 1974.*

Lubell, Cecil. **Textile Collections of the World, Vol 3, France.** *Studio Vista, London 1978; Van Nostrand Reinhold, USA 1977.*

Lubell, Cecil. **Textile Collections of the World, Vol 2, United Kingdom and Ireland.** *Studio Vista, London 1976; Van Nostrand Reinhold, USA 1976.*

O'Neill, Isabel. **The Art of the Painted Finish for Furniture and Decoration.** *William Morrow & Company, New York 1971.*

Ritz, Gislind M. **The Art of Painted Furniture.** *Van Nostrand Reinhold, USA 1971.*

Stafford, Carleton L. & Bishop, R. **America's Quilts and Coverlets.** *Studio Vista, London 1974; E.P. Sutton & Co Inc, USA 1972.*

Warin, Janet. **Early American Stencils on Walls and Furniture.** *Dover Publications Inc, New York 1968.*

Watson, Professor William (Ed). **The Great Japan Exhibition.** *Royal Academy of Arts, London 1981-82.*

Acknowledgments

The author and publishers wish to thank the following artists who, in many instances, produced work especially for this book:
The following abbreviations have been used: t top; b bottom; c centre; l left; r right.

Ian Beck - page 82.
Robert and Colleen Bery - page 62 tc.
Natalie Gibson - page 62 bl.
Magie Gray - page 62 tl and cover.
Leslie Howell - pages 84, 85, 88, 89.
Emma Guest - pages 37 t, 38, 39, 40, 41, 55, 58 tr and cover.
Lyn Le Grice - pages 80, 81.
Arthur Marshall - pages 50, 51, 53, 54.
Jane Prosser - pages 84 l, 108, 109, 110, 111 and cover.
Joy Roberts-Gray - pages 90, 91, 92.
Laurie Strange - pages 59 br, 60, 61.
Lady Rose Yorke - pages 42, 43, 44, 45, 48 and cover.

The author and publishers also wish to thank the following people and organizations for permitting their furniture to be photographed:
Sue Bodinetz - page 107 t.
Wendy Booth - pages 84, 85, 88, 89.
Moya Bowler - page 58 tl.
The English Garden - pages 32, 37 br.
Dragons of Walton Street - pages 93 tl, 93 tr, 97 tl.
Piers Gough - page 58 b.
Hippo Hall - page 97 c, 97 b.
Richard Holley - page 6.
Lady Victoria Waymouth - pages 48, 93 b.

And our most special thanks to ICI Paints Division for its invaluable help in preparing the chapter on Fundamentals.

With thanks also to the following photographers:
Richard Ball - pages 24, 25, 27, 28, 29, 31, 32, 42, 43, 44, 45, 46, 47, 49, 56, 58 br, 60, 61, 63 br, 77, 82, 84, 85, 88, 89, 107 l, 110, 112
David Cripps - pages 80, 81.
100 Idées/Duffas - pages 102, 103.
Tim Jenkins - pages 41, 48, 50, 51, 55, 58 tl, 93 br, 107 l.
Michael Nicholson/Elizabeth Whiting & Associates - page 6.
Memphis - page 99.
Ray Roberts - pages 58 tr, 62 lt, 62tr, 90, 91, 92, 93 tl, 93 tr, 97.
Tim Street-Porter/Elizabeth Whiting & Associates - page 62 b.
Studio Alchimia - pages 98, 99 b,

And to the following illustrators:
Biddy O'Grady - pages 14, 15, 17, 64, 65, 66, 67, 70, 71, 72, 73, 78, 79, 124, 125.
John Woodcock - page 105.
Jill Zeiner - pages 12, 13, 21, 22, 80, 110-119

Index